CW00816162

A Vital

A Vital Ministry

*Chaplaincy in Schools in
the Post-Christian Era*

John Caperon

scm press

© John Caperon 2015

Published in 2015 by SCM Press
Editorial office
3rd Floor
Invicta House
108-114 Golden Lane
London EC1Y 0TG

SCM Press is an imprint of Hymns Ancient & Modern Ltd
(a registered charity)
13A Hellesdon Park Road
Norwich NR6 5DR, UK

www.scmpress.co.uk

Scripture quotations are from the New Revised Standard Version of
the Bible, Anglicized Edition, copyright © 1989, 1995 by the Division
of Christian Education of the National Council of the Churches of
Christ in the USA. Used by permission. All rights reserved. And where
indicated, from the New English Bible © Oxford University Press and
Cambridge University Press 1961, 1970.

British Library Cataloguing in Publication data
A catalogue record for this book is available
from the British Library

978 0 334 05219 7

Typeset by
Manila Typesetting Company
Printed and bound by
CPI Group (UK) Ltd

Contents

Acknowledgements

I should like to thank Dr Helen Cameron, the director of the Oxford Centre for Ecclesiology and Practical Theology (OxCEPT) at Ripon College Cuddesdon during 2007–11, for the conversation in 2008 which first prompted my research into school chaplaincy. It was Helen, too, who suggested that I undertake the research in the context of the doctoral programme in Practical Theology rooted in the Cambridge Theological Federation under the direction of Dr Zoe Bennett. To both Helen and Zoe, who acted as my doctoral supervisors, I owe a great debt of gratitude for their warmth, supportiveness, occasional necessary astringency, and friendship. 'Doctorateness' was a concept – and an aspiration – helpfully clarified by Professor Vernon Trafford, who brought further warm encouragement, for which I thank him. Throughout the years in which the Bloxham Project was based at Ripon College Cuddesdon, I enjoyed not only the warm hospitality of the college's staff and students, but also the support and friendship of the then Principal, the Very Revd Martyn Percy, whose generosity and kindness I gratefully acknowledge.

The trustees of the Bloxham Project, under the wise chairmanship of David Exham, offered unstinting support for the research, which was further financially supported by the Dulverton Trust, the Haberdashers' Company, the Mercers' Company, Woodard Schools and St Gabriel's Trust. Without these resources, the research would simply not have been possible. The helpful guidance of the research reference group gave clarity and direction, so my thanks go to the Revd Professor

Mark Chapman, Nick McKemey, the Revd Samantha Stayte and Professor Geoffrey Walford. The steady hand and eye of Keith Glenny, then the Bloxham Project administrator, were central to the compilation of our database of school chaplains, as indeed they were to the smooth running and sound financial management of the whole research enterprise.

My greatest debt, though, is to the extended community of all those working as chaplains in Church of England schools. Lay or ordained, of whatever ecclesial background and in whatever school context, school chaplains are at 'the cutting edge of mission'. They are the Christian ministers most likely to have meaningful personal contact with school pupils at a particularly formative stage in their lives, in the course of what may be truly transformational ministry. So I warmly thank the very many school chaplains who over my years as director of the Bloxham Project and subsequently have allowed me to share their insights into ministry. They have been nothing short of inspirational. In particular, I want to thank the sometime chair and secretary of the School Chaplains' Association, the Revd Dr Jan Goodair and the Revd Lindsay Collins, the subsequent chair, Fr John Thackray, and the senior provost of Woodard Schools, the Revd Canon Brendan Clover. My special thanks go also to Captain David Booker CA, Fr Richard Harrison, the Revd Rachael Knapp, the Revd Dr John Seymour, the Revd Dr David Lyall, and to the Revd David Jenkins, sometime school chaplain, who first introduced me to the original Bloxham Project research.

It goes without saying that anyone writing a book needs time, space and support. These have been unstintingly given by my wife Felicity, whom I thank for her understanding and encouragement, and to whom I dedicate this work: 'a poor thing, but my own'.

John Caperon
January 2015

Introduction

Disconnected: the Church and young people

It is a truism that secondary school students in England generally don't attend church. They go – frequently and obsessively – online; they go to the shopping mall and Costa; they frequent clubs and concerts; they go – often more for social than academic reasons – to school: but they do not go to church. The cultural world they inhabit is fast-paced and immediate to their interests; it is an all-pervasive context for their thinking and feeling, and it is what largely shapes their values. The values represented by the Church – let alone the salvation story the Christian faith lives within and seeks to share with others – find little resonance with them. The young are disconnected from the Church.

There are, of course, exceptions to this general picture. Some churches do appear to succeed in attracting the young – most notably, perhaps, those in the evangelical–charismatic tradition, and located in university cities. And some contexts where the Church has adopted the cultural forms of the late twentieth and early twenty-first century – for instance the Greenbelt festival and Soul Survivor – also show a capacity to attract and keep the young on board. But broadly speaking the young and the Church are disconnected, inhabiting different worlds.

Does this matter? If the Church is content to admit that it is now a marginal social institution, increasingly of service mainly to an older and depleting population, then it doesn't matter that much: the continuity of Christian faith among the young will be confined to the niche impact made by Soul Survivor and similar expressions – and Christianity in this country will probably not

disappear but rather reduce to a tiny core of committed people, as suggested in some of the academic literature (see Collins-
Mayo et al. 2010; Heelas and Woodhead 2005).

Nor does it matter that much if we are content to see the
Christian story regarded as a clue to understanding the past
rather than as a resource for the present and future. School and
university teachers of English Literature now feel it essential
to provide religious 'background' to the classics of the literary
tradition for their students, since the imaginative and moral
worlds of Chaucer, Shakespeare and even Dickens, distinctively shaped by Christian faith, are found to be increasingly
foreign. The Christian past of our post-Christian society simply
needs to be explained, if the young are to understand huge
areas of our history, art, literature and law.

But if we want a good proportion of the young to have access
to the full range of the living spiritual resources of Christian
faith and tradition, as potential support for their current and
future living rather than for their understanding of the past,
then the major disconnect between the Church and the young
matters considerably. So what can be done?

This book argues that within the increasing number of secondary schools and academies in the church sector – not just those
formally sponsored by the Church but also those sponsored by
church-linked organizations – a key potential resource for the
Church's mission to the young is a school chaplain embedded
within the life of the school community. It also argues that the
rapidly developing ministry of visiting 'para-chaplains' – mainly
linked with local and national voluntary organizations such as
Scripture Union, and providing spiritual support for pupils in
schools mainly outside the church sector – is a dynamic further
resource offering new energy in Christian mission.

Making the connection: school chaplaincy

Chaplaincy in schools, this book argues, offers the key point of
interaction between the Church's ministry and the young – a

position the Church of England itself has not so far come to recognize. In the policy deliberation and report-writing of the early twenty-first century, there has been a strong emphasis on the significance of the Church's stake in the education system, but this has focused far more on the inherent value of holding that stake than on the purpose of the Church's involvement. And where – if at all – the ministry of chaplains in church schools has featured in the Church's official reports, there has been a combination of confused thought and false assumption, which has led to chaplaincy in schools having in effect no formal profile in the Church's missional or educational policy (see Dearing 2001; Chadwick 2012).

The origins of this book lie in my five-year tenure of the directorship of the educational charity the Bloxham Project[1] between 2006 and 2011, which followed a career in English teaching and in the leadership of church schools. Established in the late 1960s by secondary school heads and chaplains, at a time when the 'new theology' associated with John Robinson was sweeping through and both destabilizing and renewing the life of the Church, the Bloxham Project embodied a serious concern to make the Christian faith accessible to the young. It therefore set out to research the attitudes of school sixth-form pupils to religious faith and explored points of connection between the Church's faith and the lives of the young. Research outcomes were reported in *Images of Life* (Richardson and Chapman 1973), and the Project subsequently developed as a support organization for chaplains in school, its charitable objects being 'the advancement of education and of the Christian religion'.

Taking on the leadership of the Bloxham Project brought me for the first time into contact with a wide circle of chaplains in all types of school, both independent and state-maintained. Though I had acted as chaplain in the school in which I was head – with the generous support of a lay chaplaincy team – I

---

1 Since 2013 the Bloxham Project has been known as 'The School Chaplains' and Leaders' Association (SCALA)'.

had seldom met others with this role, and my new contacts were a revelation. Here were both lay and ordained Anglican chaplains from across the ecclesial spectrum, often also in the role of teacher, sharing daily school life with 11 to 15-year-olds; leading the community's corporate worship; responding to pastoral need and emergency; and advising, supporting and simply being with young people.

Researching school chaplaincy

Their narratives of ministry were compelling; their evident acceptance and popularity among pupils and their staff colleagues spoke volumes: theirs was an accessible ministry, and one that represented a Church otherwise absent from pupils' lives. It was ministry where the young were. Why, I wondered, was it not taken seriously in the Church's thinking? This prompted a decision that empirical research – the first ever – was needed into the nature, extent and effectiveness of Church of England school chaplaincy. Under the aegis of the Bloxham Project, and in partnership with the Oxford Centre for Ecclesiology and Practical Theology (OxCEPT) at Ripon College Cuddesdon, a leading Anglican theological college, I embarked on a two-year research programme in 2009.

The two-year research project embraced a range of approaches. An initial literature survey explored the field of mission, ministry and chaplaincy, revealing a dearth of written material on chaplaincy in schools. Then followed a series of scoping interviews with school chaplains and heads, designed to establish how these leading figures understood the distinctive ministry of school chaplaincy. Key questions about ministry in schools were then explored through in-depth interviews with a wide range of Anglican chaplains across the school system.

There followed the development of a database of all those we could locate working as chaplains in church schools – some 400 people – and a subsequent online survey, which drew a strong response and produced a rich cache of information about how practising chaplains understood and sustained their ministry. It was, finally, possible to interview some focus groups of students to explore their understanding of and response to chaplaincy in their schools. All the data emerging from the research was analysed for an initial, interim report presented to a national conference on school chaplaincy at Liverpool Hope University in June 2011 (Caperon 2011). Subsequently the data formed the basis of my doctoral thesis.

Beyond research – critical reflection on practice

Research produces data but data alone is meaningless unless interpreted and understood. The distinctive discipline of practical theology insists on the importance of critical, theological reflection on practice, and this book is grounded not simply in research data but in the convictions central to practical theology. It was through a process of disciplined reflection on what chaplains and others said about their ministry in schools that I developed the stance this book sets out. The central questions were 'What does the data mean?' and 'What is its significance?' In this process of theological reflection I have found particularly illuminating the idea of the four dimensions of theology: the normative (what churches teach); the formal (what theologians produce); the espoused (what adherents claim); the operant (what drives practice). This analysis, first developed in the ARCS project (Bhatti et al. 2008), has now been further explored by Helen Cameron and colleagues (Cameron et al. 2010); it is an analysis that implicitly invites reflection on how 'theory' (the formal and normative dimensions) interacts with practice (the espoused and operant dimensions). Its application to the ministry of school chaplaincy has offered key insights.

In summary, I have come to believe that the ministry of school chaplains is the most significant single point of contact between the Church and the secondary-age young. Here are people who in the name of Christ and his Church are living alongside and with the young as they explore the nature of the world in which they find themselves and develop their values for adult living. School chaplains are in the privileged position – alongside teachers – of being able to support the young in their explorations, helping them ask questions, posing alternative outlooks, challenging accepted social norms. Where chaplains are unique is in their rootedness in the spiritual tradition of Christian faith, in their concern for spirituality and spiritual development and in their representative function as 'God people'.

What this book does is to explain, and I hope justify, this central conviction of the significance of school chaplaincy as a vital ministry of the Church, and to challenge the institutional Church's apparent unawareness of this ministry's need for recognition, support and further development. I explore the cultural and religious background of the young in the early twenty-first century, and look at the efforts of Church and state to provide a spiritual dimension to education. In offering a rationale for school chaplaincy and its concern for human flourishing, I focus on its nature as understood by its practitioners and clients, also setting out the functional understanding of chaplaincy in schools, developed by the Bloxham Project. I explore the pastoral and liturgical roles of chaplains at the heart of their calling, and highlight the importance of a 'ministry of presence'. I consider some pressing professional issues for school chaplains, as well as the official policy vacuum about this ministry, concluding that the Church needs – simply – to change its attitudes and priorities if it is to meet the challenge of the disconnected young.

If the book succeeds in revealing, highlighting and celebrating the work of school chaplains in all its diversity and impact, and the significance of this ministry becomes clearer, and if we can shift – even just a little – the Church of England's inbuilt inertia, its inherent, inherited assumption that parishes are where the Church essentially operates and that chaplaincy in all its forms is a marginal and relatively insignificant sphere of ministry, then it will have served its purpose.

I

Chaplaincy: A Model of Ministry for the Present Time

Google 'chaplaincy' and there will be approaching three million results. The vast array of chaplaincy-related websites is an indication of the way this ministry has grown to prominence in recent years. It also illustrates the sheer range of what is meant by, and claimed as, chaplaincy: there are university chaplaincies, multi-faith chaplaincies, workplace chaplaincies, other-faith chaplaincies and immigrant-group chaplaincies. The sheer diversity is reflected online, and this indicates the dynamic, shifting nature of this ministry today. Since the beginning of the twenty-first century there has been a rapid and largely uncharted growth in all varieties of chaplaincy. Originally a specifically Christian ministry, it has now seen its fundamental human value both appreciated and appropriated by other faith and non-faith groups (see Ryan 2015).

In this chapter I shall contextualize chaplaincy in schools today by exploring the roots of Christian ministry and the origins of chaplaincy as a particular model of ministry. In a changing context in which both Christian, interfaith and other-faith chaplaincies are growing, and where the notion of humanist or non-religious chaplaincy is also gaining currency, I shall aim to clarify what seems to characterize Christian chaplaincy and develop a rationale for it, ending with an initial overview of chaplaincy in schools, its origins and current status.

The roots of Christian ministry

So how did chaplaincy develop as a specific kind of ministry? Answering this question involves sketching the development of Christian ministry itself. The origins of all formal Christian ministry lie in the life of the early Church and its diverse communities around the Mediterranean world, where local ministerial leadership emerged in each new church community as a consequence of the spreading apostolic mission (MacCulloch 2009, p. 9; Chadwick 1967). It seems clear that ordained Christian ministry was originally rooted in the calling to serve, and it appears to derive directly from the pattern set by Jesus. According to Mark's Gospel, 'the Son of Man came not to be served but to serve, and to give his life a ransom for many' (Mark 10.45). 'Ministry' meant self-giving service to others and participation in the – risky – leadership of the Christian community. The impulse to serve can be seen as a key part of the ethos of the early Church as a whole, though particularly located and exemplified in its commissioned, ordained ministers.

The Church's early development of a formal, authorized ministry with specific roles of deacon, presbyter/priest and overseer/bishop set a pattern of both practical, diaconal service and of recognized community leadership. This pattern would ensure both the maintenance of regular eucharistic worship in Christian communities and the sheer survival of Christian faith in the centuries before the legalization of Christianity throughout the Roman Empire under Constantine in AD 313. Over the post-Constantinian centuries, the idea of ministry as *local* service exercised a shaping influence, and eventually took institutional form in the emergence of the role of parish priest once the territorial organization of the Church and country into parishes became established by the early mediaeval period.

The poet Geoffrey Chaucer's portrait of a parish priest, 'a poor parson of a parish', written in the final decade of the fourteenth century and convincingly drawn from life, if idealized, suggests how this role – at its best – could genuinely serve ordinary people and their needs through offering spiritual leadership and pastoral care. Against the background of what he saw as a venal institutional Church, corrupted by worldly wealth and covetousness, Chaucer offers the picture of a parish priest who is a 'good religious man', characterized by self-giving generosity and committed to visiting the sick and caring for those suffering misfortune even at the furthest point of his parish. He taught Christ's gospel, says Chaucer, and first followed it himself – a model of what today would be called 'performative faith'.

Chaplaincy as 'ministry where people are'

The parish system, clearly established by Chaucer's time, rooted itself deeply in the English context. The core idea was that there should be in every local parish a place of worship (a church building) and a person (a priest) to lead worship and as an educated – or at least literate – 'clerk' or cleric to guide the spiritual lives of the parishioners. It is difficult to imagine English history and life without the institution of the parish and of the 'parson', and the landscape of the country still bears witness to the vast resources ploughed over the centuries into the provision of places of Christian worship. But with the growth of a more mobile, networked, secularized, multi-faith context in the twentieth century, the early mediaeval pattern of local ministry was less evidently suited to contemporary purpose.

Reflecting on this twentieth-century 'passing of the local community', the Roman Catholic theologian Karl Rahner wrote: 'the Church's mission has never simply moved between the local community and the local parish as its beginning and its end . . . besides the territorial basis there have always been other sociological facts forming the natural foundation for Christian communities' (Rahner 1963, p. 68). By the end of the mediaeval age, in fact, formal Christian ministry had already been exercised not only through the role of parish priest but also through the emerging role of chaplain – an ordained minister providing spiritual care and leading worship within a household or another specific, gathered community.

By the seventeenth century, chaplains are known to have been present in royal courts, aristocratic households, ships, colleges, hospitals, overseas colonies – in short, wherever people were gathered in community for a common purpose. Chaplaincy was in effect emerging as a complementary model of ministry to that of the local parish priest. Equally concerned with leading community worship and supporting and guiding the lives of community members, the associational chaplaincy model was providing ministry in contexts other than the local parish, wherever people were gathered for specific purposes and activities. This was ministry in the gathered community, ministry in the meeting place or workplace rather than in the place where people happened to reside. It was a model, simply, of ministry where people are.

So what is a chaplain?

A standard, late-twentieth-century academic definition of the role of chaplain was: 'a clergyperson who has been commissioned by a faith group or an organization to provide pastoral service in an institution, organization, or governmental entity' (Hunter 1990, 2005, p. 136). Such is the rapidity of change, though, that in the few years since this definition was coined it has become substantially outdated. Even if we limit the term to *Christian* chaplaincy, it is now no longer true that all those who work as chaplains are clergy or are formally commissioned by their faith group: some parish clergy, for example, may develop entirely informal and ad hoc chaplaincy roles in organizations within or beyond their parishes, while chaplaincy exercised by lay people has now become widespread.

Equally, the range of current Christian chaplaincies is simply not covered by the description of their context as 'an institution, organization, or governmental entity'. Chaplaincies today cover a huge range of contexts, and beside the long-established Church of England chaplaincies to areas such as education, the armed forces, healthcare and prisons, current roles also include, for example, chaplain to a local farming community, shopping-centre chaplain, chaplain to older people, chaplain to the local police, chaplain to a football club – and the list could go on. In addition to the range of traditional chaplaincies overviewed in *Being a Chaplain* (Threlfall-Holmes and Newitt 2011), there is now the far more ad hoc development of a wide range of chaplaincies in varying community contexts, recently researched and charted for the first time (Slater 2013).

The most up-to-date research on Church of England chaplaincy (Todd et al. 2014) reveals an uncertain picture, largely because, the authors argue, there is simply no conceptual clarity about what exactly constitutes the ministry of chaplaincy and no accurate diocesan or central Church of England statistics are kept for it. However, they estimate that around 1,500 ordained ministers currently serve in formally identified chaplaincy posts, nearly all of whose work is paid for by the organizations in which they minister (this representing a significant proportion of those engaged in formal Church of England ministry). Beyond this, suggest the authors, there is a significant number of 'invisible' lay volunteers making a major contribution to the provision of chaplaincy.

But in the early twenty-first century, as I have suggested, the word 'chaplain' is also being used extensively beyond its original church context. In particular, other-faith and non-faith groupings now employ the idea of chaplaincy. Humanist chaplains, for instance, have been in place in some universities in the USA since the late 1970s, and non-religious chaplaincy services are now available in some English contexts. Humanists, ironically, express reservations about the 'Christian connotations' of the word, as do some other faith groups, yet they still have their own 'chaplains' because 'people understand what they do'. The word has become a shorthand description of 'a job which people understand', says the British Humanist Association (see Crace 2010). It seems clear that the term 'chaplaincy' carries a valued freight of ideas about supportive pastoral practice.

A chaplain, then, from any faith or non-faith group, could today be described as 'a person designated by a sponsoring organization to offer care and support to members of a group or community'. The appropriation of both the title and some aspects of the role of 'chaplain' by other-faith and non-faith groups can be seen as a very positive indication of how valuable a model Christian chaplaincy has become for those in other communities. There appears to be a general, human need that chaplaincy responds to, beyond what simple friendship and other human relationships can provide. We could describe this need as one for reliable, trustworthy, personal support, encouragement and guidance, offered in a spirit of self-giving service.

If chaplaincy is to be *Christian*, however, it clearly has to retain the 'religious connotations' that humanists want to discard. Instead of accepting a secularized, de-sacralized understanding of its role, Christian chaplaincy needs to be understood as taking its identity and motivation from its origins in the practice of Christian ministry, combining both diaconal service and spiritual leadership. And crucially, it is a pastoral ministry carried out in the name of Christ and his Church. Christian chaplaincy, therefore, is a distinctive ministry: rooted in the tradition of authorized Christian ministry, it is now a sphere in which both lay and ordained ministers work, but it remains essentially a ministry to people where they are in the workplace or community, one that offers pastoral support and spiritual guidance and leadership to those who for whatever reason or need seek it.

Pastoral care and human flourishing

The idea of 'pastoral care' needs elucidation. The word 'pastoral' is, of course, deeply rooted in the Christian tradition: a rich vein of Old Testament imagery sees God as the pastor or shepherd of his people, the one who protects and guides them. 'He will feed his flock like a shepherd', wrote Isaiah (40.11); and the shepherding image runs through the Psalms, as in Psalm 23: 'The LORD is my shepherd'. Inheriting this image, Jesus is said to have had compassion on the crowds, since they were like 'sheep without a shepherd' (Matt. 9.36); and the image of Jesus as the 'good shepherd' is prominent in John's Gospel and developed in its final section where Peter is charged with the responsibility to 'feed my sheep' (John 21.17). The language of 'pastoral' care is at the heart of Christian ministry.

But pastoral care – rather like chaplaincy – requires a robust Christian definition beyond its current secular understandings. The practical theologian Stephen Pattison has consistently argued for such a 'strong' definition, and offers the following in his *Pastoral Care and Liberation Theology*: it is 'that activity within the ministry of the Church which is centrally concerned with promoting the well-being of individuals and communities. The ultimate aim of pastoral care is that of ministry as a whole . . . to increase love between people and between people and God. Its specific functions are healing, sustaining, reconciling, guiding and nurturing' (Pattison 1997, p. 14). This robust understanding of pastoral care is a world away from the kind of 'niceness' pilloried by Giles Fraser (Fraser 2014); it presupposes a world in which evil, injury and hatred thrive, and have to be confronted and changed.

Closely related to Pattison's notion of human 'well-being' is that of 'human flourishing' (a term he also uses), and these both require further specifically Christian clarification. Questions about the nature of human happiness and what constitutes the 'good life' are, of course, perennial; common to them is a question about the nature of the human person, and it is in this area that Christian thinking needs to be clear. Theological anthropology – understanding the human in the light of God – suggests two possible but profoundly contrasting Christian approaches to human nature: the Augustinian and the Irenaean, both of which assume the spiritual, God-created nature of humanity. In the Augustinian vision, argues John Hick, there is little place for the idea of human development or growth in goodness. However, the notion of human potential is at the heart of the Irenaean vision (Hick 1974).

Irenaeus focuses less on an understanding of humanity's fallen nature than Augustine, and asserts our potential, through divine grace, for change, development and goodness. For Irenaeus, the 'image of God' within us is real; and we are truly 'made in the image of a reality that is both personal and relational' (Spencer 2002). In the light of this understanding, there is real substance to the idea of human flourishing: it becomes more than simply vague, humanistic aspiration; instead, it reflects a spiritual vision of human destiny, summed up in Irenaeus' words 'the glory of God is a man fully alive, and the life of man is to see God' (Irenaeus, *Against Heresies*, Book 4, 34:5–7). John's Gospel, after all, speaks of Jesus coming to give 'life . . . in all its fullness' (10.10, NEB), interestingly in the 'pastoral' context of the image of the 'good shepherd'. So 'well-being' can convey an ideal of 'life to the full', of human harmony (a notion of the whole, integrated person, spiritually aware and responsive to others and to God) – an ideal towards which the work of ministry in pastoral care is directed. At the heart of Christian chaplaincy, therefore, as a pastoral ministry of care, is the possibility of 'flourishing'; ministerial service is not offered as a merely superficial sticking plaster for the injuries and hardships of life but rather as a potentially transformative service of love and care that will assist the person more fully to develop his or her God-given potential in relationship.

Pattison is rightly concerned to identify the link between pastoral care and liberation theology. Arguing that pastoral care is in danger of being – or even often actually is – confined simply within an 'individualistic therapeutic paradigm', where the aim is to secure individual healing, he suggests that true pastoral care exists in a socio-political dimension in which the individual person is recognized as living within society, where he or she may be experiencing oppression and where liberation theology insists on its first function as seeking liberation from that oppression. Pattison's particular concern is with the situation of people suffering mental illness and of women experiencing social, personal or sexual oppression; but what the young of the post-millennium generation may be experiencing as oppression is of a different, more complex sort, as the next chapter will indicate.

So in the light of this we could define the aim of pastoral care in the ministry of chaplaincy as seeking the liberation of all people from what oppresses them, by bringing to bear on their lives the love of God expressed in and through Jesus Christ, and enabling them to live in harmony with others and with God. This is an understanding of human flourishing that is not just about the individual, and certainly not solely about the individual's material circumstances, but is a holistic vision of the person at peace – the Old Testament vision of *shalom* is powerfully relevant – with him or herself, in community and with God. Pastoral care has a challenging implicit intention: to foster in the name of Christ the well-being and human flourishing of all; and chaplaincy's agenda is through pastoral care and spiritual leadership to nurture the well-being and human flourishing of the community in which the chaplain is situated.

The identity of Christian chaplaincy today

The idea of the flourishing community raises the issue of eligibility and extent: who is eligible for the Church's pastoral care, and for whom is it intended? The practical theologian Martyn Percy offers thinking on this subject that is helpful in clarifying further the identity of Christian chaplaincy. Discussing models of ministry in the rural context, Percy proposes that we think in terms of contrasting 'intensive' and 'extensive' models of ministry, where 'intensive' suggests ministry focused on the needs of the gathered church community and 'extensive' suggests ministry offered and extending to the wider, whole-parish community. A parallel contrast, he argues, is that between 'market' and 'utility' understandings of ministry. A 'market' view implies that ministry and pastoral care are to be seen almost as commodities in a marketplace, to be offered and 'bought' by people; whereas a 'utility' view suggests that pastoral care is a common right or entitlement for all rather than for a few who choose to 'buy in' (Percy 2013, p. 43).

This is an illuminating model when applied to chaplaincy ministry. If we can see the whole community in which a chaplain ministers as being the sphere of his or her ministry, rather than simply the responsive or needy individuals within it, then there is a fascinating comparison with the role of the traditional rural parish priest discussed earlier. It is not a question, that is, whether people in their designated sphere of ministry 'buy in' to the chaplain's services. All are assumed to be entitled to them, whatever their personal faith standpoint or degree of religious commitment: the chaplain is there for each member of the community, just as Chaucer's 'poor parson' was. To use Percy's categorization, we can therefore describe the ministry of Christian chaplaincy as essentially built on an 'extensive/utility' model. It is implicitly a genuinely inclusive ministry.

To summarize so far, I have argued that the general notion of chaplaincy has now been widely adopted in secular and other-faith contexts, where the role has been described both (disparagingly) as a kind of 'professional nice guy' and (very much more positively) as one that cares for 'the spirituality of human beings' (Threlfall-Holmes and Newitt 2011, pp. 123, 135). However, I have also argued that there is a specific content to *Christian* chaplaincy. Here is a ministry that is identifiably carried out in the name of Christ and his Church; can be traced back to the 'servant' calling of Jesus and to the earliest models of formal ministry in the Church; takes its impulse from the traditional role of Christian pastoral care-giving; is offered inclusively to the whole community; and aims to promote human flourishing so that all may attain their God-given potential.

Chaplaincy and the Church's mission

How is this ministry of chaplaincy located within the wider mission of the Church? Recent missiology has focused on the idea that the mission of the Church is the mission of God. In other words, what God is doing in the world – sustaining, renewing and redeeming all creation – is what the Church has to collaborate with, since 'God is already ahead of us in mission' (Avis 2005, p. 8). Drawing on the landmark thinking of the Second Vatican Council's *Lumen Gentium*, which considers the mission of the Church, and its key statement that God has 'generously poured out his divine goodness and does not cease to do so' (Abbott 1966, p. 585), the theologian Paul Avis sees mission as simply: 'the overflowing of the love of God's being and nature into God's purposeful activity in the world' (2005). At the heart of this kind of theology of mission is a realization that the human world is interpenetrated by the divine presence; it is a vision of the world itself and human life as being sustained by an ongoing 'overflow' of dynamic, divine love and goodness.

This, however, raises the question of how we evaluate human culture. In his ground-breaking *Christ and Culture*, the German–American theologian H. Richard Niebuhr explored what he saw as the wide spectrum of differing Christian understandings of the relation between 'Christ' (the divine) and 'culture' (the human world). Identifying two extreme polarities, one view which sees human culture as in opposition to Christ and the other which sees Christ expressed in and through human culture, Niebuhr argued persuasively that human culture was capable of being a vehicle for the divine (1951). This idea of the potential of the human to mediate the divine lies, of course, at the root of a theology of incarnation as well as a theology of mission: it is a belief in the ultimate goodness of God and the ultimate salvation of the human through the divine incarnation.

Given the Irenaean conviction that the image or *ikon* of God is and remains present in humankind, and that the human may mediate the divine, there are clear consequential implications for a theology of mission. Among these are that humankind has the potential through grace for ultimate fellowship with God; that our very human personhood – a personhood realized and fulfilled in relationship – is itself derived from God as Trinity; and that the Incarnation displays in Jesus Christ the true image of our humanity. The core implication of 'image of God' theology is that humanity, and each human person, is precious: loved eternally by God, redeemed by God and capable of relationship with God, a destiny that points beyond time and space.

Avis argues that the Church's ministry is 'defined by mission' but rightly insists that the Church is not, as he puts it, 'in the futile business of attempting to bring an absent Christ to an abandoned world', since God in Christ is not absent from the world, nor is the world abandoned by God: the human world is interfused, as Niebuhr argued, by the divine. The work of God and the work of the Church are essentially identical, the Church being called to continue and replicate the mission and ministry of Christ. In this way of thinking, Christ is both present in the worship of the Church – the celebrant at every Eucharist – and is the impulse driving every act of service performed by the Church. The mission of the Church could therefore be described, in brief, as to continue the work of Christ, to be Christ to the world.

The Church's calling to be Christ to the world is exercised through its ministry of word, sacrament and pastoral care – and this has to be seen as a corporate mission of the whole Church, not just the preserve of those ordained to its formal ministry. In this economy, chaplaincy – pastoral ministry where people are – has a particularly significant part to play in the present age. With the decline of geographical community as the main reference-point of people's lives, and the increasing importance of 'community' as an experience rooted in commonality of interest or activity, in association, in networks and gatherings, chaplaincy comes into its own. The traditional model of the parish church as the fixed centre of ministry to a surrounding local community looks increasingly archaic, nostalgic, less and less convincing. Chaplaincy – and not least chaplaincy in schools – needs by its very nature to be at the heart of the Church's mission in the twenty-first century.

The origins and development of chaplaincy in schools in England

Given this understanding of the nature and significance of Christian ministry today, I shall turn now to sketch the origins and development of chaplaincy in schools. It can be traced back to the mediaeval era, when all educational institutions were in effect under the control of the Church, and all teachers were clergy. Education then took place in a highly religious context, almost as a by-product of religious practice, and pupils would have lived under a semi-monastic regime. It is unclear exactly when the role of chaplain emerged as differentiated from that of teacher, since all teachers were clerics; but as one historian of Christian education has insisted, 'godliness and good learning' were inextricably linked (Newsome 1961, pp. 32–3).

By the nineteenth century, however, the role of chaplain had emerged in the old 'public' schools, and by mid-century it was widely and clearly established in these schools and in the rapidly increasing number of new independent schools, being seen as a role carrying powerful spiritual and moral influence. The mid-Victorian school story *Tom Brown's Schooldays* (Hughes 2008) provides one interesting insight, drawn from life if somewhat idealized, into the influence on the members of Rugby School of their chaplain–headmaster Dr Arnold. As the public schools grew and new independent schools were established, so more chaplains were appointed. They would conduct daily Anglican worship in their school chapels, teach the Christian faith in divinity classes and act as personal advisers to pupils. They combined the core ministerial tasks of leading worship, teaching and pastoral care.

By the early twentieth century the place of 'chapel' and the chaplain in independent school life were central, and the chaplain was a leading member of the school staff. It was not until after the Education Act of 1944, however, that chaplaincies began to be replicated in the newly created state-maintained church secondary schools. By no means all of these new schools appointed chaplains, but the common independent school pattern of a chaplain who would also be head of religious education – or divinity – appears to have been echoed in many of them.

By the end of the twentieth century, chaplaincy had become a feature of several parts of the English school system. Broadly, all the traditional Anglican independent schools continued to have chaplaincy provision, some of the more prestigious schools developing multi-faith chaplaincy provision alongside their resident, Christian chaplaincy. In Roman Catholic secondary schools in England, both private and state-maintained, the provision of chaplaincy was universal, though the late-twentieth-century decline in the numbers of priests and religious meant that many Roman Catholic maintained schools now had female lay chaplains, which in turn meant that the central act of worship – the Mass – could only be celebrated by a visiting priest.

By the second decade of the twenty-first century, Church of England state-maintained secondary schools – including the recently increased number of Church-sponsored academies – presented a mixed and uncertain picture of chaplaincy provision. The Bloxham/OxCEPT research project completed in 2011 identified just under 400 school chaplaincy roles in England, Scotland and Wales, encompassing both private and state-maintained sectors, and received survey responses from 218 chaplains. By the time of the Church of England's report *The Public Face of God* (Camp 2014), 198 Anglican state-funded secondary schools were identified in England and Wales, all of whom were asked to respond to a chaplaincy survey. This most recent study drew responses from just 72 schools (a mere third of the total number), from which no clear pattern or model of Anglican chaplaincy in schools emerged. The lack of clear information about chaplaincies identified in Andrew Todd's and Victoria Slater's 2014 study (Todd et al. 2014) is replicated here.

From the available sources, however, we could summarize the current situation as follows. Some church schools employ chaplains (lay or ordained) on a full-time basis with no teaching commitment; others – predominantly the independent church schools – employ the traditional chaplain/teacher model; others have visiting chaplaincy provided by a local clergy person or a group of local clergy, sometimes set up ecumenically; some employ 'Christian youth workers' as chaplains – the standard pattern in one diocese; and yet others have no school-based provision but rely on local churches or charities to provide occasional, visiting chaplaincy services. The picture, in brief, is both diverse and complex.

One new and dynamic feature of schools' chaplaincy is the emerging provision of para-professional 'chaplaincy' services to non-church schools from a number of voluntary sources, mainly of interdenominational, evangelical provenance. Organizations such as the Luton Churches Educational Trust (LCET) have a strong local record of supplying educational and pastoral support for local schools, through off-site courses to build student self-esteem, through RE teaching and assemblies in school and through personal befriending understood as 'chaplaincy'. My reservation expressed in the inverted commas around the word is simply that while chaplaincy as an authorized ministry of the institutional Church has a clear theological and practical identity, as I have sought to demonstrate, it is as yet unclear what are the driving theological impulses behind LCET and similar related organizations. I shall explore this issue in more detail in Chapter 8, but my sense is that they may be impelled more by an evangelistic than a disinterestedly pastoral impulse, adopting something more akin to 'intensive' and 'market' paradigms of ministry than the inclusive extensive/utility pattern identified above. Is this genuinely chaplaincy? In the current context, it is arguable that what is claimed as chaplaincy must have at least some title to its identity (Ryan 2015).

Conclusion

In this chapter I have argued that chaplaincy is pre-eminently a ministry for the present time, one whose social relevance is indicated by the fact that other-faith and non-faith groups are now developing their own versions of it. Surveying the origins of chaplaincy as a development from the Church's earliest pattern of ministry, I also considered the specific nature of Christian chaplaincy today, identifying its core activity as pastoral care and its aim as the flourishing of the human person in community and in relationship with God, and drawing particularly on the practical and liberation theology perspective of Stephen Pattison to support this stance.

From this I developed a theological rationale for chaplaincy, rooted in the conviction that the Church's mission – comprising the work of both lay and ordained people – is about sharing the mission of God, and the work of Christ in care and service, with people where they are gathered, through a ministry of word, sacrament and pastoral care. In turning finally to the ministry of school chaplaincy I sketched the origins and current status of this ministry; in the next chapter I shall set out the situation of those of secondary school age in the post-millennium era. Describing the wider, cultural context will illuminate the need of the young for a spiritual dimension to their lives so that they may have access to 'life in all its fullness' and to genuine 'human flourishing'.

The Cultural and Religious Context for School Chaplaincy

What is the cultural and religious context in which young people of the post-millennium generation live in the early twenty-first century? How does this context impact upon them and how conducive is it to human flourishing? I begin this chapter by exploring how we might best characterize our current situation, and I look at some of the relevant social, cultural and religious evidence. I then attempt to describe the current 'world' of young people, consider some of the issues faced by this generation and suggest how the young relate to inherited patterns of church and religion. Without 'engaging with contemporary culture' (Percy 2005) it is difficult to understand either the needs and aspirations of the young or the nature of the challenges and opportunities involved for those working in school chaplaincy.

A post-Christian society

Easter 2014 saw the Prime Minister both declaring his personal affiliation to the Church of England and arguing that the UK remained 'a Christian country'. This brought an immediate riposte from a group of leading atheists who in a letter to the *Daily Telegraph* argued that Britain was a 'non-religious' society and that attempts to characterize it as 'Christian' would engender 'negative consequences for politics and society' and even 'alienation' (BBC News 2014). The subsequent public furore indicated that the question remains a live one. On the one hand, some argued that church attendance was so minimal that it was absurd to claim the country as 'Christian'; on the other, some referred to the 2011 Census, which saw 59 per cent of respondents still claiming Christian allegiance. To enrich the debate, leading representatives of other-faith groups in the country declared their support for the Prime Minister's stance, arguing that while their own faiths had a proper place in British society, it was still correct to call the country as a whole 'Christian'.

The Easter 2014 debate reflected the increasing social impact of the anti-religious lobby, what has amounted since the beginning of the new century to an all-out assault on religion by the so-called 'new atheists'. Their uncompromising book titles – *The God Delusion*, *Against All Gods* and *God is Not Great: How Religion Poisons Everything* (Dawkins 2006; Grayling 2007; Hitchens 2007) – indicate their polemical determination. Their argument was that the terrorist attack on the New York twin towers on September 11 2001 had made clear the true, ferocious nature of religion, and this needed to be opposed in the name of science and reason. Various Christian responses highlighted what were seen as the fundamentalist scientism and rampant irrationalism of the new atheists (McGrath and Collicutt 2007; Beattie 2007), while other apologists sought to place religion in the forefront of humankind's search for meaning, and of our awareness of an 'otherness' beyond apprehension (Armstrong 2009).

The 'debate about God' occupied centre-stage for the first decade of the new century; and no moderately aware sixth-form student or teacher of religious studies could avoid it. That it should resurface in the second decade was indicative both of the determination of the atheist lobby and of the ongoing persistence of religion. As the literary and cultural critic Terry Eagleton has argued in *Culture and the Death of God*: 'the Almighty has proved remarkably difficult to dispose of', going on to suggest that religion has proved easily the most tenacious and universal form of popular culture (2014). Whether or not that is the case, theism and atheism remain hot debating topics.

The secularization debate

The Easter 2014 debate also reflects the ongoing academic controversy over secularization theory, the idea that there is a tendency at work in society – secularization – which means that both the institutions and the practices of religion inevitably lose their social significance over time. The most apocalyptic among recent proponents of this view, Steve Bruce, posited in his starkly titled *God is Dead* a process of religious decline beginning in the West with the sixteenth-century Reformation and leading inevitably to the present time, an era of 'disenchantment'. Today, he argued, all measures of religious practice – church attendance in particular – indicate that the Christian culture, which over more than a thousand years has dominated Britain, is 'in serious trouble' (2002, p. 60). In another depressingly titled book, *The Death of Christian Britain*, Callum Brown explored the process of secularization over the two centuries leading up to the millennium and located the point of 'no return' in the early 1960s. 'From 1956 all indices of religiosity start to decline', he argued, 'and from 1963 most enter free fall' (2001, p. 188).

But other writers have attacked secularization theory. The Canadian philosopher Charles Taylor argued against the 'master-narrative' of secularization: although its proponents saw secularization as a linear, irreversible process leading inevitably to the end of religion, Taylor asserted the 'reconstitution' of religion, the view that 'in religion, nothing is lost' (2007). The English sociologist Grace Davie, similarly, has argued for the persistence of the sacred in contemporary society despite the undeniable decline in churchgoing (1994, p. 94), noting that what needs explanation is not so much the disappearance of religion as its surprising persistence. In a related way of looking at things, some writers describe this perceived 'persistence of the sacred' as 'latent' or 'implicit' religion (see Bailey 1998); and others have proposed a process of the 're-enchantment' or 're-sacralization' of our society following its earlier 'disenchantment'. Some observers have begun to speak of a new 'post-secular age', highlighting this factor (Rowson 2014).

One major study, *The Spiritual Revolution* (Heelas and Woodhead 2005), looked at religious practice in the Cumbrian town of Kendal and concluded that a fundamental process of change was going on, in which the practice of the Christian religion was giving way to a new, non-confessional 'spirituality', a subjectively focused and individually expressed kind of post-religious phenomenon where people say: 'I'm not religious, but I am spiritual', and even create networks for 'spiritual but not religious' (SBNR) people like themselves. Heelas and Woodhead argued that we are no longer in an age in which organized religion can provide structures for life and answers to its problems; instead, the present is a time for subjective spiritualities through which each person can find his or her own way.

The sociological and philosophical arguments will doubtless continue, as will the debate about God and the more political debate about whether – and to what extent – we remain a 'Christian country'. An illuminating coda was added by the former Archbishop of Canterbury, Rowan Williams. Interviewed by *The Telegraph* after Easter 2014, Williams said: 'If I say that this is a post-Christian nation, that doesn't mean necessarily non-Christian. It means the cultural memory is still quite strongly Christian. And in some ways, the cultural presence is still quite strongly Christian. But it is post-Christian in the sense that habitual practice for most of the population is not taken for granted' (Moreton 2014). This characterization of the country's condition as 'post-Christian' – rather than post-secular – seems both accurate, helpful and nuanced. The Church of England and its ministers – including school chaplains – operate in what is best described for practical purposes as a post-Christian context: only a cultural memory and a diminishing Christian cultural presence remain.

Features of the post-Christian age: the multi-faith dimension

This is reflected in declining church attendance. Different estimates indicate that between six and fifteen per cent of the population may currently attend church regularly; but an estimate of future 'church membership' – a more complex category than simple 'attendance' – is that by 2020 it will have fallen to less than a tenth of the population (Brierley 2014). Some project a mere three per cent of the population attending church by 2030 (Heelas and Woodhead 2005, p. 148). Equally, the 2011 Census figure of 59 per cent of respondents claiming adherence to the Christian religion shows a steep decline from the 2001 figure of 72 per cent: strong, downward trends are currently evident.

The religious picture in the UK, simply, is changing rapidly. Not only is there a sharp decline in claimed Christian adherence between the 2001 and 2011 Censuses, there is a sharp rise in those claiming 'no religion' from 15 per cent to 25 per cent of respondents. If we look at under-fives, the 'no religion' figures reported by their parents increase: 34 per cent of under-fives were recorded in this category. Also significant is the fact that in the 2011 Census almost five per cent of respondents described their religion as Muslim; and again, looking at under-fives, that figure increases: of the under-five population of the UK, nine per cent are described by their parents as Muslim. Other minority religious groups – Hindu, Sikh, Jewish and Buddhist – represent altogether a relatively stable four per cent of the population.

It seems clear that while numbers of minority religions other than Islam are stable or increasing slowly, there is a sharp downward trend in claimed Christian adherence and a sharper decline in actual church attendance, alongside a steep rise both in Muslim allegiance and in the numbers of those claiming no religion. And as the 'no faith' and Muslim populations burgeon, the age profile of the churches continues to rise. The survey data for the Westminster Faith debates – a series of public debates on the place of religion in society established in 2013 – indicates a progressive detachment from Church of England adherence as people get younger (Westminster Faith Debates 2014). In effect, Christian ministry is now set in a dynamic climate of change in a post-Christian and multi-faith context.

Features of the post-Christian age: international uncertainty

What is the global context of Britain's post-Christian, multi-faith society? The new century and millennium began with a burst of fireworks and optimism on millennium day, 1 January 2000, and for some it genuinely felt as if the world had changed, had even been renewed. I shared some of those feelings, since it was the day on which my first granddaughter was born; but it was not long before the optimism of the new millennium began to fade. By September 2001 things were beginning to look very different: '9/11' marked a new stage in world affairs. The 'war on terror' was unleashed: within a month American troops began the invasion of Afghanistan; and in March 2003 the USA and UK invaded Iraq. The optimism of the new millennium was past: instead of Fukuyama's 'end of history', the supposed universal triumph of liberal Western democracy (1992), the new century had ushered in a new age of instability.

The first decade of the century saw wars in Iraq and Afghanistan. These were followed by the uprisings of the so-called 'Arab Spring', unsettling the earlier stability of the Arab states of North Africa and the Middle East. The long-drawn-out and hugely destructive sectarian civil war in Syria from 2011 created a vision of the ongoing destruction of a whole nation, and potentially of other neighbouring states; and out of the chaos of Syria emerged the chilling ideology and apparently unstoppable rise of the so-called Islamic State. By late 2014 the whole Middle East was once more a cauldron of instability and violence, with a further destructive Israeli campaign against Hamas having taken place in Gaza. In Europe a kind of new Cold War was returning, prompted by the Ukraine crisis, the Russian annexation of the Crimea and Russian-led destabilization and civil conflict in Eastern Ukraine. The international order felt more unstable than at any time since the Cuban missile crisis of 1962.

Features of the post-Christian age: economic uncertainty

To this new collection of international uncertainties, the twenty-first century has added huge economic instabilities. The fundamental, underlying macro-issues facing the global economy – how to feed and protect a vastly expanding world population in an era of global warming and unstable climate change, and how to sustain ever-expanding growth and consumerism in a world of limited resources – remain. But today's post-millennium generation of school students inherit and enter into an economic world very different from that of their later-twentieth-century predecessors. Instead of the relatively stable context of the growing Western economies of the second half of the twentieth century, with economic and employment security more or less assured, the global financial shock of late capitalism in 2008 has left a legacy of both personal and government debt and of public austerity.

The UK young now face up-front fees for university education, rising house prices and rents and significant graduate unemployment, with the pool of young unemployed around a million. This adds up to a probable future for many without housing security and with the prospect of an adult life saddled with personal debt: an Institute of Financial Studies report in 2014 suggested on average students would graduate with debts amounting to more than £44,000 (Crawford and Jin 2014). It was further reported in 2014 that just under half the 18 to 30 year-olds in Europe live with their parents, even though the figure in the UK was only 26 per cent – figures that emphasize the ongoing dependency of the young (Malik 2014). The post-millennium generation faces a debt-ridden, longer working life, considerably less generous pension provision than their parents and a consequently less comfortable eventual retirement.

At the same time, a rise in the wealth and privilege of the 'super-rich' and the ongoing persistence of an unemployed or part-employed underclass are in some ways restoring the huge social inequalities of the Edwardian era of a century ago. An

Oxfam report to the World Economic Forum in Davos in 2014 revealed that the world's 85 richest people command as much wealth as the poorest half of the world's population (Weardon 2014). And at a national level a further report shows that the five richest families in the UK command as much wealth as the poorest 20 per cent of the population (Dransfield 2014). Inequality is a growing phenomenon in the UK: while austerity measures continue to hit the poorest families hardest, a wealthy elite has seen their incomes spiral upwards.

An increasingly competitive world economy means not only tougher international competition for the UK but also a less comfortable and socially secure life than enjoyed by the post-war generations from the 1950s through to the end of the century. The emergence of the dynamic 'new economies' of the Asian and Latin American countries, the declining position of the USA and the rise of China all indicate further uncertainty ahead. For school students this means the education system, prompted by the increasing prominence of the OECD's Programme for International Student Assessment (PISA) tests, gearing itself up to higher and ever more demanding levels of attainment, with consequent additional pressures to achieve in the classroom. The race for educational qualifications has never been harder.

And all this is in a context where the basic assumption is that the Western economy should be designed so as to provide consumer goods in increasing variety to as many as possible, who may well then define themselves in terms largely of their ownership. The materialist consumerism of the early twenty-first century – dubbed 'Affluenza' (James 2007) – is culturally inescapable; advertising is ubiquitous, in all forms of media, so that one of the original biblical sins – covetousness – is now in effect the engine driving the consumer economy. For any member of the post-millennium generation to see things differently requires a considerable exercise of countercultural imagination: that things *could* be different; that life is *not* just about material possessions; that humankind simply *cannot* live by bread alone.

In our post-Christian, multi-faith context, therefore, the post-millennium generation faces the anxieties of a politically disordered world and an economy producing uncertainty of future employment and housing as well as huge disparities of economic fortune. If for the baby-boomer generation things could only get better, with rising salaries, house values and standards of living, for the latest generation the road ahead looks distinctly bumpy. The twenty-first century feels very much like a new age of anxiety.

The digital age, social media and democracy

Distinctive also of the new century is the dominance of digital technology and media: the post-millennium generation are 'digital natives'. For the digital native, digital communication has largely replaced the older, paper-based variety. The internet is the assumed source of information and purveyor of knowledge, and increasingly is at hand-held length from the student. The smartphone, carried everywhere, accesses everything the internet offers; the tablet is as natural a way to watch a film or YouTube video as a fixed device in the home. The greatest store of information that has ever been available for us is – quite literally – at hand. School programmes may try to boost awareness of the vast differences between information, knowledge and wisdom, but these distinctions may not matter that much to the young: they live with the internet and probably use rather than critique what it offers. The post-millennium generation are potentially better informed about everything than ever were their parents and teachers. As a visual information medium the internet carries a vast array of YouTube and other videos that hugely enhance its educational potential.

At the same time, this very potential has its dangers. One genre that exploits the new accessibility of the visual is online pornography, to which the internet gives instant access in a couple of clicks. For many of the post-millennium generation their understanding of human sexuality will be unavoidably influenced by this source. A large proportion of teenage boys – one study in the USA suggests over 90 per cent (Sabina et al.

2008) – will have accessed pornography online, shared it with their peers and imbibed from it both images and understandings of sexuality. The online world does not simply illustrate, it also provides meanings, in effect promoting the sexualization of the social imagination. From a feminist perspective the outcomes of internet pornography include the sexual objectification of the female as well as more male pressure on young women to conform to the body image and sexual behaviour of the pornified female. At the same time, however, there is an attempted fight-back from 'fourth wave' feminism, expressed in attempts to remove topless photographs from the *Sun* and to counteract what has been called 'everyday sexism' (see Bates 2014), a continuing phenomenon that disturbs women, distorts human relationships and is arguably as harmful to male self-understanding as it is to women themselves – a theme of the United Nations' He4She gender equality initiative.

Social media – powerful means of supporting and enhancing human relationships – are similarly ambivalent. Text messaging – and sending 250 texts a day is said not to be uncommon (Thompson 2013) – also carries the potential for 'sexting' (the sending of sexual or sexualized messages and images by phone). The smartphone makes possible the sending of intimate self-portraits between girls and boys, girls reportedly responding to male invitations and pressure to do so; posting these on the internet has become common. Facebook has reportedly now lost a following among the young, having been taken up by parents, uncles and aunts, but up to a dozen alternative social media sites are available, including Snapchat, which offers a photo-sending facility. What has been called 'the web's dark side' (Topping 2013) includes the malevolent encouragement of self-harm; and even chat sites may form a covert world not only of harmless interaction but also of personal abuse, and may also act as forums for the development of unhelpful relationships or even sexual grooming.

Digital culture has vast and ambiguous implications. It is possible to see it as undermining much of what was taken for granted in earlier times, for instance: that published information could generally be assumed to be reliable; that some information should be subject to restriction; that respect and confidentiality are at the heart of all good human relations. But despite all this, and despite the potentially grim implications of a pornography-tolerant society, the digital revolution has brought a massive degree of cultural democratization, where anyone can blog or tweet, anyone can access all the internet's information and any-one can post comments on news items or other articles. And developments in the 'big data' field – notably the growth of MOOCs (open-access online courses) – offer the opportunity of distance-learning education to anyone anywhere with an internet access device.

The twenty-first century: an age of oppression?

What does all this mean for the post-millennium generation? And what moral and spiritual qualities are needed to live well in this context? Christian faith and ministry have traditionally been concerned with the good life, a vision of abundant living, human flourishing or 'life in all its fullness', as I argued in the previous chapter. But for the current younger generation this ideal may not be easily realized. Huge forces shape events and society in ways that impact directly on their lives and construct the kind of world in which they will live their adulthoods. The digital world in which they are naturally at home pro-vides space for self-expression but is also a potential context for bullying and oppression: it cannot be seen as a benign place. The schools in which the young learn are increasingly preoccu-pied by the push for higher academic attainment, in the face of which other, less quantifiable but more personal and spiritual aspects of education may be marginalized: the development of character and resilience – traditional educational goals – may suffer.

Living well in the twenty-first century seems to demand con-siderable emotional intelligence and the capacity to be mor-ally discriminating, to make wise and discerning choices. The

Irenaean vision sketched in the previous chapter – 'the glory of God is a man fully alive' – encourages us to see the divine potential of human beings made in the image of God; but as we look at the twenty-first century context it seems clear that the future lives of the post-millennium generation will not be easy. They are subject to a range of potentially oppressive forces that will limit their opportunity to experience 'fullness of living' as they grow towards, into and through adulthood.

This may contribute to the unease and lack of well-being identified as a characteristic of the lives of the young in the new century. Anxiety and depression are reportedly common, affecting as many as a fifth of our young people. The *Good Childhood Report 2013* noted that 'about 20 per cent of eight to 15-year-olds score below the midpoint for psychological and/or subjective well-being, while 10 per cent, or half a million children, score low on both measures and could be said to be struggling' (The Children's Society 2013). And the Prince's Trust reports that more than one in five of those from deprived homes (22 per cent) believe that 'few' or 'none' of their goals in life are achievable, compared to just five per cent of those from affluent families (The Prince's Trust 2011). It has also been reported that ChildLine was in 2014 talking with more children than ever before about suicide.

The UK performs poorly in international league tables of well-being. A UNICEF report in 2007 placed us at the bottom of a table of 21 developed countries for overall child well-being. Findings from a later report include comparatively high rates of teenage pregnancy and numbers of young people out of education, employment and training. We have one of the highest alcohol abuse rates among 11 to 15 year-olds; and the report also notes that despite our moving up the league table in overall well-being, since 2010 the UK downgrading of youth policy, and cuts to local government services, are having a profound, negative effect on young people aged between 15 and 19 (UNICEF 2013).

Symptoms of a lack of well-being among the young are not hard to find. Self-esteem and body-image anxieties, uncertainties about the future and a sense of purposelessness fostered by – among other things – the existence of self-harm and suicide-related websites and blogs are reported to be undermining the confidence of many. It would be unrealistic to suggest that the whole of the post-millennium generation is afflicted; but the anxieties created by an age of personal responsibility and choice, by an uncertain future and by the constant pressures of the online world and of a consumer culture are real, and they do not seem to make for human flourishing and well-being.

Well-being, resilience, faith and identity

The term 'well-being' needs some clarification. One academic study adopted an approach to the concept that explicitly includes the spiritual dimension, and explores well-being by look-ing at four key domains relating to young people's relationship with themselves; with the community; with the environment; and with the transcendental (Rees et al. 2005). This study indicates that those respondents who identify as having a religious affili-ation were inclined to have a stronger sense of purpose, and to score more highly across all domains of well-being than others. A sense of purpose – provided by religious affiliation, involvement in prayer and belief in eternal life – may be a strong factor in young people's resilience in facing life, it concludes. The key idea of resilience has been further explored. A review of the academic literature on young people's well-being, resilience and spirituality in times of austerity (Sharma and Hopkins 2013) highlights the significance of religion and spirituality in helping young people to cope during austere times and in providing them with a sense of identity and purpose. It seems that social research helpfully con-firms what Christian and other religious groups have intuitively known: that resilience, or coping with life, is central to well-being and also linked with a faith-related sense of purpose.

The teenage years are widely recognized as the time when young people generally acquire or confirm their personal identity, their sense of values and purpose and what the developmental psychologist James W. Fowler calls a 'master-narrative' – an ideology or worldview – that will shape their subsequent living. Discovering and developing one's personal identity – in Fowler's terms, 'the struggle for identity vs role confusion' (Fowler 1981, p. 77) – is not likely to be an easy process in the post-Christian age whose characteristics have just been outlined. Pressures abound: the pressures of the peer group, of the materialistic culture of consumerism and fashion, of advertising and the media – all of which are 'selling' a master-narrative of their own, which is to do with body-image, material success, possession, dress, shopping. The 'haul video' – a genre in which young women display via YouTube posts the 'stuff' they have recently bought – might well symbolize this narrative.

The young – disconnected from the Church

The Church has traditionally been a repository of resources for living. It provided a range of supportive elements: spiritual wisdom embodied in scriptural and traditional teachings about how to live; religious practices of prayer and worship intended to raise the heart to God and to provide structure and meaning to life; frameworks of discipline (confession, absolution, penance); and sources of counsel and advice, within the church community or within its formal ministry. As long as the young were in touch with the Church's teaching and practices, these resources could be called upon in the adolescent process of seeking identity and purpose. Church Sunday schools and youth work once mediated these resources to substantial numbers; but there is now an alarming disconnection between the Church and the young.

A church growth research project undertaken for the Church of England between 2011 and 2013 reported that nearly half the Anglican churches in the UK have fewer than five under-16s in attendance (Archbishops' Council 2014); and affiliation statistics

gathered for the recent series of Westminster Faith Debates show a
devastating pattern of lower age groups being increasingly disconnected from the churches and from Christian faith (Westminster
Faith Debates 2014). Broadly, therefore, the post-millennium
generation is unchurched; and anecdotal evidence indicates that
for a secondary school student in a non-church school to admit
to attending or being even vaguely connected with the Church
is to be seen as 'weird'. While there are indications that for some
minority-ethnic Christian students their church may be a place
where both their ethnic and Christian identities are affirmed, for
the mainstream young, 'church' remains outside their experience.

What does this mean for the spirituality of the young? Large-
scale attitudinal surveys undertaken over the past 30 years provide a background, demonstrating clearly a growing distance
between the young and the attitudes, values and practices of
the churches (see Francis and Kay 1995; Francis and Robbins
2005). Two small-scale research studies into youth spirituality
were published by the Church of England in the first decade
of the new century. The first, *Making Sense of Generation
Y*, explored whether popular culture could provide a locale in
which the young could encounter God. The research revealed
that traditional religious stories and concepts were simply not
part of young people's frame of reference; they had no salvation story or master-narrative. Instead their worldview was
based on the 'happy midi-narrative', an understanding of life
with no reference to the divine and incorporating a belief that
'the universe and the social world are essentially benign and life
is OK' (Savage et al. 2006, pp. 37–8).

Subsequently, *The Faith of Generation Y* explored the beliefs of unchurched young people, concluding that socialized
into an adult world where Christian faith is marginal to living,
they are broadly unconnected to religious tradition or practice.
The researchers did however identify an 'immanent faith' or
'bedroom spirituality' – a non-confessional, personal reflectiveness that might help the young in their task of constructing
an identity. But the distance of the young from the spiritual resources the Church represents is plain. One interviewee

quoted says: 'I love me and my family and friends. No other Gods. I believe in myself' (Collins-Mayo et al. 2010, p. 33). This sense of self-sufficiency, of the needlessness of a divine or transcendent dimension, may be characteristic of the stance not only of those researched for this study but of the post-millennium generation as a whole.

A generally religiously disconnected generation is also pictured in the sociological symposium *Religion and Youth*. While this offers evidence of the continuing impact of some spiritual practices, such as pilgrimage, on the young, and of the continuing influence of religious heritage on the young of minority faith groups, the underlying argument of the book is plain. The sociologist of religion Linda Woodhead summarizes it like this: 'that religion is no longer transmitted down the generations; that the historic churches have suffered dramatic decline; that Christianity has lost its cultural monopoly; that duty and deference have been supplanted by individuality and authenticity; and that the young are invited by the culture to "forge their own unique identities" (Collins-Mayo and Dandelion 2010). One young woman quoted in *Religion and Youth* offers what feels like a definitive, generational view: 'I believe in things like love and stuff like that, feelings, more so than religious things. I don't have any beliefs on that side at all' (Day 2010, p. 99).

The young: spiritually unresourced, lacking spiritual capital

Disconnection from the Church means that the post-millennium generation are not able to draw on the religious heritage of the Church and its spiritual resources. This means that there is a kind of spiritual deficit among the young, what we might think of as a dearth of spiritual capital. Lacking a sense of the transcendent, a context of inherited faith, the young are having to find their identity and purpose without the resources that previous generations have had in the spiritual experience embodied in the Judaeo-Christian tradition and mediated to them through the continuing cultural presence of the Church. For in this post-Christian era, the Church is in effect culturally absent from the lives and consciousness of the post-millennium generation, however strong the lingering 'cultural memory' of Christianity may be for some older people.

The idea of spiritual capital refers to what we inherit or acquire as spiritual resource from the religious tradition; and it can be seen as both a personal and social resource. I shall consider in a later chapter the link between worship in church schools and spiritual capital, but for the moment it is sufficient to consider it in relation broadly to the post-millennium generation. The young – in an age of anxiety and potential oppression – are no longer able to draw on the bank of religious tradition from which they have become disconnected. Yet that tradition remains a potential source of story, vision, values and spiritual energy that could animate the lives of the young. In the next chapter I shall look at the ways both Church and state see the education system as providing a source of spiritual capital for the young.

3

The Spiritual Dimension:
The Response of State and Church

In the previous chapter I sketched the social, cultural and religious context in which the post-millennium generation live – an
age of considerable anxiety – and identified the disconnection
between this generation and the Christian tradition. I argued
that this disconnection leads to a spiritual deficit or dearth of
spiritual capital among the young. In this chapter I shall describe
the now dwindling attempts of the national education system
to provide an element of spiritual resource for the young, and
shall look at the special contribution of the Church of England
through its provision of a distinctively Christian education in its
own schools. I shall explore how the Church understands the
mission of its schools and look at how chaplaincy is currently
seen within them, arguing that this ministry is ideally placed to
contribute significantly to school ethos and to the spiritual
dimension of education and to enabling the young to access spiritual capital. Chaplains, I shall argue, can play a leading part in
developing the religious literacy of school students, socializing
them into the religious world; and they can offer the personal
and pastoral support that will nurture spiritual development.
But at the very time when the young are in need of spiritual
support for their personal development, the Church seems to
be neglecting to provide an essential resource – chaplaincy in
schools – to minister to them.

The 1944 settlement and school worship

From the beginning of English state-maintained education in 1870 a key principle was that all children should receive 'religious and moral training' (Maclure 1965, p. 137). The Education Act of 1944, which established the 'dual system' of county (i.e. state) and voluntary (i.e. mostly church) schools, reinforced this. Local education authorities were charged with providing education that would contribute towards the 'spiritual, moral, mental and physical development of the community'. This specific commitment to the priority of the spiritual dimension was expressed in two ways: in the requirement that each day in every school should begin with 'collective worship', and in the provision of 'religious instruction' in all schools (Maclure 1965, p. 224). Trust deeds in independent church schools made similar provision: in effect, the spiritual dimension of education was to be delivered in England via the Christian religion, whose spiritual capital could be accessed by all.

The post-1944 generation therefore experienced a school regime in which a religious dimension was clearly present, both in the classroom and in daily worship. As part of that generation I experienced a religiously-shaped primary education. In my church primary school, each day began with worship, the partitions between classrooms drawn back to make a space large enough for the school to gather. We sang hymns from Ralph Vaughan Williams' and Percy Dearmer's *Songs of Praise*, heard readings from the Gospels in the Authorized Version and said the Lord's Prayer together daily. In religious instruction we learned Bible stories, and there were special services in the local parish church on festival days. A significant degree of cultural Christianity was part of the ethos of my – and in all probability many others' – primary school experience.

In secondary schools things were probably very different. As secularity spread from the 1960s onwards and religion began to lose its public and social significance, 'assembly' in many secondary schools deteriorated to the point where it was little more

35

than a ritual of social control. A context for corporate discipline, the affirmation of the school's social values and the recognition of sporting success, secondary school assembly now had little overt religious or spiritual significance. Some secondary schools – notably church-maintained schools and independent church schools – continued to offer a religious dimension for their students through worship in the school chapel. But as the cultural revolution of the 1960s continued, and the habit of deference was replaced by the assertion of individual values, even religion in the public schools itself could become seen as outdated, a feature of the oppressive past to be excised, as in Lindsay Anderson's cult film *If...* (1968).

However, the immediate post-war generation emerged from its experience of collective worship in schools – particularly in church primary schools – probably knowing some Christian prayers, having sung some of the best-known Christian hymns and being familiar with core Bible stories and with the life and teaching of Jesus. It also absorbed a – broadly – common set of values based on the Judaeo-Christian moral tradition: a source of spiritual capital. This, rather than any large-scale, popular churchgoing, is likely to be the origin of the cultural Christianity referred to in the previous chapter. Similarly, classroom religious instruction (later to become religious education, and later still religious studies) contributed to cultural Christianity, providing for the post-war generation a certain familiarity with basic Christian concepts – God, faith, virtue, evil, salvation, judgement, mercy – and an insight into religious practice.

School worship today

By the 1970s and 1980s the picture was very different, as the school system reflected the growing secularity and increasing diversity of wider society. The Christian hegemony of the 1940s, 1950s and even 1960s was a thing of the past. In the overwhelmingly secular culture of the state comprehensive I taught in during the 1970s, 'collective worship' played no part and religious education had become absorbed into the wider context of a humanities programme. At the start of the day the emphasis was on tutorial rather than assembly time, with tutors giving personal attention to students' work and personal lives. Occasional assemblies were held to celebrate achievement or give the opportunity for students or staff to share their passions or concerns; but the focus had shifted from God, religion and the transcendent to ourselves and our community: an illustration of the 'massive subjective turn' of Western culture identified by Charles Taylor (1991).

What is remarkable is that some 70 years on from 1944, the requirements for collective worship and religious education are still on the statute book. More recent legislation even sets out a specific obligation to adhere to Christian norms in school collective worship: the 1988 Education Reform Act provides that collective worship should be 'wholly or mainly of a broadly Christian character'. This appears strange in the light of the wholesale changes in the cultural and religious make-up of the population between 1944 and 1988 and the growing multi-faith and post-Christian nature of our culture during that period. It looks like deliberate resistance to cultural change, as if legislators wanted consciously to safeguard the Christian cultural heritage of the nation in the face of an increasingly multi-faith and secularized context.

But it is entirely unclear how many schools in fact meet the legal requirements. In 2004 Ofsted reported that over three-quarters of secondary schools (76 per cent) were not complying with the law and were not conducting collective worship; and David Bell, then Her Majesty's Chief Inspector of Schools, argued on this basis that the obligation of collective worship should be abandoned. In 2011 a survey showed that fewer than a third of pupils nationally (28 per cent) took part in a daily act of worship (Accord Coalition 2014). If only around a quarter of pupils nationally in both primary and secondary schools take part in collective worship, it looks very much as if the 1944 and 1988 legal provisions now have limited effect. Despite the continuing existence of legislation that in theory keeps a place for religious worship in the state-maintained education system, in practice it has since 1944 been slowly leached from the nation's schools.

Efforts continue to remove the legislation altogether from non-church schools, while leaving schools of a religious character free to conduct worship. The National Governors' Association (NGA), representing 300,000 school governors, issued a statement in 2014 seeking to abolish the 1944 requirement for collective worship, arguing that 'schools are not places of worship but places of education'. In response a senior church figure called for 'widespread debate', arguing that a 'time of spiritual reflection' in schools, drawing on all the world's great spiritual traditions, would be more honest and in tune with contemporary culture than collective worship, and would be less anachronistic than requiring people to worship, which was by definition a voluntary activity (Holness 2014a; Holness, 2014b). In practice it is likely that church schools are increasingly the only schools to include collective worship as an element in the spiritual education of their students.

RE and collective worship today

The educational status of religious education (RE) has also declined over time. In the early years of this century, religious studies (RS) as both a GCSE and an AS/A level subject displayed burgeoning popularity, although it could be argued that advanced syllabuses increasingly focusing on philosophy and ethics were encouraging little understanding of religious experience, belief or practice. Even so, the recognized presence of the subject in the examination system was significant, and arguably safeguarded a place for faith and thinking about faith-related issues. This accounts for the despair expressed by many RS teachers in the second decade of the century when RS was not included among the newly defined EBacc subjects – thus reducing considerably the numbers choosing to study it at GCSE level and also thereby A level take-up.

So – in summary – what seems clear is that beyond the primary phase, where remnants of religious worship may persist in many schools, most secondary schools now operate on a largely secular basis. Nor is evidence from school inspection encouraging as far as religious education is concerned. An Ofsted report of 2013 based on observation of RE in some 200 schools found that too many pupils were leaving school with low levels of subject knowledge and understanding and that even most GCSE teaching seen failed to enable pupils 'to adopt an enquiring, critical and reflective approach' to the study of religion. At the same time, RE in primary schools was found to be 'inadequate' (Ofsted 2013) – an alarming situation in a multi-faith context where basic religious literacy seems an essential requirement for all.

So the 'average' secondary student in a state-maintained, non-church school is unlikely to experience collective worship of any resonance or depth, and the quality of RE is likely to be uncertain. In effect, the religious element prescribed in 1944 is now likely to be missing from the education of the great majority of school students, certainly in the secondary phase. Church schools, both independent and state-maintained, appear to be pretty much the only places where religious worship continues as a reliable feature of school life, and where RE/RS is given curricular priority as a core subject. However, even in church schools, things are not as they might be. A review commissioned by the Church of England Board of Education found that RE was good or better in just 70 per cent of church-maintained secondary schools and academies, and found the subject in need of improvement in more than half of church primaries (Holness 2014c).

The spiritual dimension?

None of this means, of course, that the *spiritual* dimension of education is necessarily being ignored in the nation's schools. One problem with the spiritual dimension – an aspect of 'spiritual, moral, social and cultural education' (SMSC) – is that of definition: what exactly is meant by 'spiritual' education? An Ofsted report of 2004 acknowledges that 'of all experiences, it is the spiritual which . . . is most resistant to operational definition'. The same report, however, goes on to set out helpfully what might be considered under the heading 'spiritual'. Included are: insights, beliefs and values; the search for meaning and purpose; self-knowledge and empathy; appreciation of the intangible and mysterious. In this context the report goes on to suggest that a working definition of 'spiritual development' would be that it is 'the development of the non-material element of a human being which animates and sustains us' (Ofsted 2004).

It is far more difficult to assess how well schools are promoting the spiritual development of students, understood in this way, than to assess whether collective worship is taking place or whether RE is being well taught. But there remains some hope that all young people may develop at least elements of spirituality through the experience of their school curriculum. The creative subjects of art, music and drama (like RE also regrettably sidelined by the EBacc) do give real opportunities for students to enter the world and vision of others, and can encourage the development of both empathy and self-knowledge – two of the components of the spiritual noted by Ofsted. The 'arts' subjects can similarly nurture human understanding: both history and geography can enable students to grasp something of the reality of the lives of people of other times and other places. The imagined worlds and lives accessed through poetry, fiction and drama can also contribute to the development of empathy, insight and understanding. And science and mathematics are capable not just of offering explanation and calculation but also enabling students to gain a sense of the astonishing complexity and wonder of the created universe.

But for the school curriculum as a whole to open up the spiritual dimension requires an imaginative and bold educational vision. The education system's core assumptions, however, are currently more to do more with 'output' in terms of test and examination results than with an overall vision that acknowledges and embraces the spiritual. Instead it seems likely that academic subjects are seen by most teachers and pupils as separate silos of knowledge and skill rather than as aspects of a unified understanding and vision, together nurturing a human wholeness which includes the spiritual dimension. Examination statistics are easier to read than the spiritual condition of a school community and its individual members. In effect, the nation's state-maintained non-church schools may now be offering a depleted education: one that lacks a unifying, comprehensive vision of 'life in all its fullness', of human flourishing.

The distinctive nature of church schools

What is different about church schools? A brief factual perspective will be helpful in exploring this question. Following 1944, voluntary schools – mostly Anglican and Roman Catholic – represented a significant proportion of the state system, and this remains true. Just over a quarter (4,386) of our near 17,000 primary schools are Church of England schools, with other Christian denominations, mainly the Roman Catholics, accounting for a further 1,750 or so. Only a tiny minority of primaries have other-faith allegiance: 33 Jewish schools, six Muslim schools and three Sikh schools. Of some 4.3 million primary pupils, just over 800,000 are in Church of England schools, with around half that number in Roman Catholic schools and a further 20,000 in other Christian schools. What is striking is that in this strongly secular and multi-faith age, more than a quarter of primary pupils are still taught in Christian schools.

In the secondary phase the picture is different. Of 3,281 schools in all, there are only 208 Church of England schools and 323 Roman Catholic schools; other Christian schools number 77, with ten Jewish schools, eight Muslim schools and one Sikh school. There are 186,845 pupils in Church of England secondary schools and 311,430 – approaching double that number – in Roman Catholic schools, with 73,640 in other Christian faith schools. So out of some 3.2 million secondary pupils, just under a sixth are taught in Christian schools, with (again) tiny minorities in other faith schools; 7,490 in Jewish schools, 3,725 in Muslim schools and 1,325 in a Sikh school (Department for Education 2013).

What these figures show is that in a society hugely changed since 1944 and now predominantly post-Christian, secular and multi-faith in identity, the churches – and certainly the Church of England – still hold a substantial stake in the state-maintained education system, as also remains the case in the independent sector. It is in these church schools that the spiritual dimension of education and a concern for the whole person, for character and resilience, have a special place. Unsurprisingly, however, the existence of church schools has been contested since at least the 1980s, and secularists have argued for the abolition of all 'faith schools' – legally 'schools with a religious character' – on the grounds that that they foster social and cultural division. Church schools especially have been lambasted since they are seen as offering a covert selective mechanism into a privileged haven from the multi-cultural reality outside for the children of Christian – often seen as white and middle class – parents.

The Church has firmly defended itself against such charges, highlighting the inclusive nature of its schools and its determination to maintain its stake in the system. A number of arguments have supported this. *The Fourth R* (Ramsey 1970) suggested that whereas Roman Catholic schools had a 'domestic' purpose, designed to provide a Catholic education for Catholic pupils, Church of England schools were simply provided as an aspect of the Church's service to the wider community. When secularist attacks on church schools first erupted in the 1980s, this liberal line of argument became seen as inadequate, and more robust thinking developed. By the 1990s a far more assertive understanding of their purpose and identity had emerged among church schools, much of which became crystallized in the Dearing Report, *The Way Ahead: Church of England Schools in the New Millennium* (Dearing 2001).

Dearing: a rationale for distinctive church schools

Dearing was in effect the first serious attempt to provide a rationale for the Church's continuing involvement in education through its schools. The report offers far more than simply a defence of the territorial status quo, and has a significant theological and missiological basis, arguing that church schools are central to the mission and outreach of the Church since 'church schools reach out to the young in far greater numbers than regularly attend church'. A clear strategic realism marks the whole report, which defines the purpose of the Church in education as: 'to offer a spiritual dimension to the lives of young people . . . in an increasingly secular world' (Dearing 2001, pp. 3–4). This is the fundamental claim: that church schools make the spiritual dimension their priority and are thus centrally concerned with mediating spiritual capital.

There is no theological hesitancy about Dearing. The million or so children and young people in Church of England schools are, says the report, 'being given the opportunity to know Christ, to learn in a community that seeks to live by his word, and to engage in worship'. The justification for church schools 'lies in offering children and young people an opportunity to experience the meaning of Christian faith' (Dearing 2001, pp. 10–11). Church schools are now seen as having both domestic and general functions for, respectively, church adherents and for other parents. Their inclusivity is asserted, as is the centrality of school ethos – the belief that 'Christian values and principles will run through every area of school life'. Pupils do not just learn about religion but actually experience 'a living tradition and inheritance of faith' (pp. 12, 13).

Dearing marked a newly assertive approach by the Church. Instead of being able to rely, as in the past, on having a secure and accepted place within the education system, the Church would in a multi-faith, secular age now have to define and defend the distinctive nature and purpose of church schools and justify their position in the national educational economy. This it does powerfully. Yes, argues Dearing, the Church of

England is indeed providing particular kinds of school; they are distinctively Christian; the Church does give special priority to the spiritual dimension of education; and all our pupils will experience the 'living tradition' of faith within the school. That is what we offer, and in an age of cultural diversity and of parental choice we have no hesitation in asserting that specific identity.

Church of England schools and chaplaincy

This was hugely significant, and certainly a strong enough prospectus on which to ground the report's vision – since increasingly realized – of the founding of further church secondary schools. But there are two odd things about the Dearing Report. The first is its sidelining of the oldest church schools in the country, those founded by the Church or Crown or by later charitable effort, and which are now in the independent sector of education. Although independent schools overall educate a mere 7 per cent of the age cohort, their influence is disproportionate to their numbers; and it was in these schools, as I have shown, that the work of school chaplains began and where it still remains a core part of educational provision. Dearing does urge the Church to 're-engage' with church schools in the independent sector, but as a whole the report glosses over their continuing socially and culturally significant role specifically as church schools. While this may be politically understandable, the Church being reluctant to highlight its links with socially privileged schools, it remains unfortunate.

More fundamentally, Dearing fails to deal in any serious way with the unique contribution chaplaincy can make to a church school's life and ethos. The report concedes that the distinctive identity of a church school may be 'enhanced . . . by a chaplaincy' (Dearing 2001 p. 19), but this indicates a complete failure to grasp the potential significance of the ministry of a chaplain. For talking about the mission of church schools without considering chaplaincy is like trying to describe the life and mission of parishes without mentioning the role of parish priest, or simply suggesting that having a priest might 'enhance' a parish. In the one paragraph of the report that specifically concerns chaplaincy, Dearing notes that a 'significant number of church schools have a chaplain'; but the mention of 'financial considerations' as a limiting factor really means that chaplaincy is just not seen as a priority (p. 56).

The fact is that one of the key elements in the ethos and identity of a church school and its life as a Christian community – the Christian pastoral ministry of a chaplain – is simply sidelined by Dearing. There is a crucial omission in this important policy document; and the more recent Chadwick Report, *The Church School of the Future* (Chadwick 2012), similarly sidelines chaplaincy. Concerned largely with strategic and structural issues in an era of the marketization of the education system, and with how best to secure the Church's stake in education for the future, this report also asserts the importance of a distinctive Christian ethos in church schools but fails to recognize how chaplaincy might make a decisive contribution. What is a key ministerial provision for supporting the spiritual dimension of education is simply overlooked.

A different approach: chaplaincy in Roman Catholic schools

The Roman Catholic Church, in contrast, is clear not only about the priority of the spiritual dimension in education but also about the centrality of chaplaincy in the mission of its church schools. The goal of Roman Catholic education has been described as 'drawing out the potential in each person to the full, in a community which recognizes the centrality of Christ as our guide and inspiration' (Hume 1997, p. 33). So education is concerned with the whole person and with his or her personal formation: hence the school is a place of academic learning within the context of spiritual life; the spiritual aims of education have de facto centrality.

From this deeply theological vision of education as personal formation – the fostering of character, spirituality and resilience – follows naturally the role of chaplain as someone whose special concern is not with the subjects of the school curriculum but with the whole spiritual dimension of education, with the community's spirituality and with the development of each person's spiritual life. Across a range of normative Roman Catholic theological sources – canon law, episcopal statements, official documents from the Catholic Education Service and dioceses – the Church sets out a powerful vision of chaplaincy in schools. The chaplain represents the 'centrality of Christ'; helps each member of the school community to 'become more aware of God's presence and to empower them to celebrate that presence' (Archdiocese of Southwark 2007); becomes a companion 'to every member of the school and college community to help them embrace and further the memory of Jesus and his Word' (Catholic Education Service 2004). The chaplain 'recognizes the face of Christ in each member of the community and treats them with respect as people who share in the life of God and are unique and of infinite value' (Diocese of Portsmouth 2009). It is a compelling vision.

This theology of chaplaincy foregrounds the idea of companionship, of spiritual accompaniment, something that emerges strongly from a personal account of chaplaincy in Roman Catholic comprehensive schools in the north-east. In her ironically titled *Wasting Time in School*, Sister Mary McKeone highlights this ministry of accompaniment, describing her work as encouraging young people to reflect on their development and spirituality, to pray, and to 'deepen their perception of God in their lives'. School chaplaincy, she says, is about 'lavishly giving quality time to pupils in quiet listening' (McKeone 1993). This powerful vision is one that coalesces perfectly with an understanding of the school as above all a place of spiritual growth and of personal formation.

In fact much of the thinking in the Dearing Report really echoes this Roman Catholic commitment to holistic, formative education with an evident priority for the spiritual dimension.

What Dearing fails to identify is the clear – even obvious – link between a spiritually focused educational vision and school chaplaincy. Dearing recognizes the essential nature of the educational enterprise – offering a distinctive, faith-based education which affirms the spiritual identity of the human person – but has drawn back from recognizing the significance of the key, ministerial element in providing it. Roman Catholic theology, in contrast, sees what Dearing calls 'the centrality of Christ' as personally embodied in the presence and ministry of the chaplain in school, who is charged with nurturing the spirituality of all.

Spirituality and school ethos

If chaplaincy holds a key responsibility for the community's spirituality, as this theology insists, the Christian ethos of the school must be one of its main concerns. Dearing is insistent on the place of ethos, 'a living tradition and inheritance of faith', though the word itself is never emphasized. Dearing may well have avoided a term of uncertain definition, but educational researchers have explored the nature of school ethos and helped define it more substantively. Caitlin Donnelly shows that ethos is not simply located in a school's formal statements but rather in concrete social interaction – how people behave to one another (2000). Terence McLaughlin sees ethos as 'the prevalent or characteristic tone, spirit or sentiment' of a school, whose influence is seen in 'the shaping of human perceptions, attitudes, beliefs, disposition and the like' (2005, pp. 311–12).

From this perspective the idea of ethos resonates with the French sociologist Pierre Bourdieu's notion of *habitus*, which he describes as 'the deep-structured cultural dispositions within a community or an institution, which are part of primary socialization and habit-formation' (McLaughlin 2005, p. 314). In the light of this understanding we can see school ethos – an amalgam of a school's implicit values, priorities, relationships and way of being – as a central, formative factor in the development of young people and their spirituality. School ethos is thus a prime agent of religious socialization, to be understood not as a form of indoctrination but rather as an introduction to the way of faith; something for pupils to be invited to understand and to consider as a possible pathway for their own lives.

Spiritual development and the spiritual journey

The 'pathway' image brings a further dimension to the notion of spiritual development with the metaphor of the 'spiritual journey'. This often-used term suggests that our human spirituality is not essentially static but dynamic, and that it is a God-given aspect of our humanity that can grow and develop as our lives continue. Something similar is suggested by J. W. Fowler in his understanding of faith (or spirituality) as 'people's evolved and evolving ways of experiencing self, others and the world' (1981, p. 92). The key word here is 'evolving': faith and spirituality tend not to stand still, although as Fraser Watts and colleagues point out in *Psychology for Christian Ministry* (Watts et al. 2002), it is important to recognize that people will not necessarily 'progress' straight through Fowler's stages of faith to a 'higher' or 'more developed' stage.

Fowler's idea of 'stages of faith' or of spirituality is nevertheless helpful in understanding the spiritual development or journey of young people, and can be a sharp tool of analysis, assisting pastoral practice by helping a chaplain or counsellor gauge how best to support a particular student in crisis or distress. For it is clear that during their teenage years members of the post-millennium generation will be going through the process of developing their own spirituality, and that many will face personal, family and life issues that will be difficult to negotiate, as I suggested in the previous chapter. The journey through the teenage years is from the perspective of the church school not just a process of personal and academic development – a growing understanding of the world and how to relate to it – but primarily a spiritual journey, one in which the young person may be supported within the clear faith context provided by the school community's spiritual life, drawing on the resources of the Church's spiritual capital.

Conclusion

In this chapter I have described how the state education system has since the 1944 Act gradually withdrawn from offering, through collective worship and RE, the religious resources that could provide spiritual capital for young people in non-church schools. In looking at the distinctive nature and place of church schools I have highlighted their concern with providing for students 'a living inheritance of faith' through a school ethos that can act as a means of religious socialization; but I have also noted the contrast between Roman Catholic schools where chaplaincy is central and Church of England schools where it is sidelined. As the post-millennium young confront the issues of their own adolescence and its questions of personal identity in an age of anxiety, and as they explore beliefs and values in the search for meaning and purpose, a school chaplain may be, as Roman Catholic thinking suggests, a companion on the way, a spiritual guide, a sounding-board for thinking and exploration. The Church of England secondary school should surely similarly offer chaplaincy to support the process of spiritual development: a personal ministry of support and accompaniment responsive to all in the process of their growth towards fullness of life.

4

A Ministry of Presence:
What School Chaplains Offer

In the previous chapter I looked at the spiritual and religious dimensions of English education, identifying the dwindling impact of collective worship and RE in most schools and singling out church schools in the independent and maintained sectors as places where serious efforts are still being made to ensure a spiritually resonant education for students. Noting the Church of England's strange official sidelining of school chaplaincy and contrasting this with the positive vision held by the Roman Catholic Church, I explored the potential for chaplains to be major contributors to school ethos and to the spiritual development and identity formation of students, acting as companions of the young on their spiritual journey.

I shall now turn to the ministry of chaplains in church schools: what do they offer to the young and also to other members of the extended school community? The practical theologian Paul Ballard has recently written about the nature of chaplaincy ministry (2009, p. 152), developing the idea of the chaplain as 'embedded' in the institution or community in which he or she serves, as in some recent conflicts journalists have been 'embedded' with the armed forces. The implication is that the chaplain is living in and alongside the community and yet working to a value system extending beyond it, even counterculturally. Chaplaincy in schools can helpfully be seen in this light. The full-time chaplain is 'embedded' in the school to minister in the name of Christ to all members of the extended school community – pupils, teaching and non-teaching staff, parents and governors – any of whom may need the support of a chaplain in relation to personal, family or institutional matters. As I argued in my opening chapter, chaplaincy is ministry where people are, in the context of their daily lives and activities; and in a school, the whole of the extended, working community is the 'parish' to which the chaplain ministers.

In this chapter, therefore, I shall try to describe what this whole-community ministry of school chaplaincy looks and feels like from the perspective of practitioners. It was the practitioner perspective that was the focus of the Bloxham/OxCEPT research project of 2009–11, the first practical-theological research undertaken into this ministry, which I described in the Introduction. The personal perspectives of school chaplains were specifically sought so as to extend our understanding of how these chaplains experience their ministry, and what they are seeking to be and to do as they carry the responsibility for Christian ministry in the school as the 'public face of God' (Camp 2014). In what follows I shall both draw on the Bloxham/OxCEPT research data and correlate it with other theological insights to present a picture of school chaplaincy in practice.

Being a chaplain in school – role and identity

But a prior caveat is needed. In discussing Christian ministry we need to recognize that service and care are callings for all Christians and not intended to be the preserve of those who are ordained. Any community in which a chaplain ministers will probably include other practising Christians as well as people of other faiths or of no faith. But while the lay Christian is asked to live Christianly, she or he is not called to public service and witness in the same way as a chaplain. Many schools – given the long tradition of teaching being seen as a vocational occupation – will contain some teaching staff who are practising Christians, and in church schools we might expect that many will be. Again, many schools will include pupils who come from Christian homes, even if they are in small numbers; and in church schools the proportion of these pupils may be significant. But it is only the chaplain whose role in itself declares a specific faith commitment: so a term such as 'the public face of God' or – to put the issue even more starkly – 'the God person' describes the core element of the chaplain's role and identity.

The two words 'role' and 'identity' point, however, to two contrasting ways of seeing chaplaincy, and I shall look first at the idea of role. This word could misleadingly suggest the playing of a part, an external appearance or series of actions 'put on', as an actor might put on a costume for a stage part. In using the word I want to be clear that I am describing simply what is externally visible, what is actually done and performed, what the chaplain's social functions amount to. During the course of the Bloxham/OxCEPT research programme we identified several functional aspects of the school chaplain's role, and it will be helpful at this point to introduce that analysis. In the opening chapter, looking at the origins of ministry, I described the core elements of Christian ministry as service or pastoral care, and liturgical leadership, and these two dimensions are perhaps inevitably at the heart of what school chaplaincy is about. But our research revealed the school chaplain as having a complex and multi-functional, multi-faceted role, a full description of which would include at least all the following elements:

- Pastoral: caring for the whole community.
- Liturgical: leading prayer and worship.
- Spiritual: leading the spiritual life of the community.
- Missional: commending the Christian faith and supporting faith groups.
- Prophetic: 'speaking truth to power'.
- Pedagogic: teaching about faith, and Christian catechesis.

I shall explore these various dimensions of chaplaincy in the school context later, but for the present it is helpful just to note that chaplaincy in schools goes far beyond pastoral care, even where we take a really 'high' definition of pastoral care as 'attending to and nurturing' others 'for God's sake', as Stephen Pattison has expressed it (2008, p. 9). The role of the school chaplain is indeed complex and multi-dimensional.

The centrality of 'being'

But another way to consider chaplaincy in schools is to look at identity, going beneath and beyond the external functions the chaplain performs to her or his personal identity. What the Bloxham/OxCEPT research project brought out powerfully was the way school chaplains from widely differing ecclesial backgrounds and ministerial contexts see their personal identity and being as the real heart of their chaplaincy. The chaplains we interviewed and surveyed characteristically described their work in personal rather than functional terms. They spoke of 'making Christ present in school', 'being the presence of Christ in the school' or 'being the visible presence of the Church'. It is as if the chaplain is particularly conscious that it is in and through who he or she genuinely and authentically is that the presence of God in Christ is made known and publicly declared.

This recalls a profound theme in catholic thinking on priesthood, namely the idea of the priest as an *alter Christus*, another or 'alternate' Christ, one who stands in the place of Christ to bring his message and presence to others. From a sociological and functional viewpoint the focus is on the priest's service to his community; from a sacramental and ontological viewpoint the focus is on the priest's personal identity or being (Benedict XVI 2009). Translating this into the context of Church of England school chaplaincy, we could say that research reveals chaplains holding an 'espoused theology' of chaplaincy that resonates strongly in this respect with the formal theological thinking on priesthood of the Roman Catholic Church (see Cameron et al. 2010). Anglican school chaplains are specifically conscious of their calling to be 'God people' in their community.

A 'ministry of presence'

Chaplains interviewed for the research project, and those responding to our survey, both highlighted this idea of a ministry of presence. At its simplest level this is about physical presence in the community: 'being there and being around'; 'roaming purposefully'; or even just 'loitering', as some of them described it. One chaplain spoke self-deprecatingly of 'engaging in a kind of desultory hanging around'. This suggests that the sheer presence of the chaplain is itself felt to be significant, to mean something beyond itself: the chaplain is a sign or signifier. One chaplain saw himself as a 'representative symbol of spiritual values', another as being 'a physical expression of Christianity', saying 'ultimately I'm a little Christ here . . . I do believe I'm trying to take God's presence into the classroom and into the hallways and into the playgrounds.'

It isn't part of this kind of vision to believe that the 'hallways and playgrounds' are a kind of godless sphere, however. It is more that a chaplain carries the special consciousness that she or he is 'the public face of God', recognized by others in the school, both staff and students, as being the one whose special calling it is to evoke the divine, to suggest the transcendent, to represent God. In the following accounts, school chaplains reflect on what this role as the 'God person' means for them. First, a lay teacher-chaplain in a suburban church academy writes about the practical dimensions of his 'ministry of presence':

My ministry of presence is utterly dependent on my being seen as present in and around the academy community. If I am not present, being obviously visible and available, how will staff and students know they can approach me to chat and talk about the issues they face? In practice, this means I try to be visible and available at the beginning and end of the day, in breaks and at events where students and parents come into the school.

There is something deeply incarnational about the role of a teaching chaplain, living and working as an identified

Christian alongside colleagues. As Chaplain I am the representative of both the wider Church, and in a very real sense, of God, to the students and staff of the Academy. For many I will be the only Christian minister who they regularly see and speak to. But only if I make time to be present.

This chaplain's emphasis on being 'visible and available' in the academy is characteristic of the thinking of other school chaplains and also conveys a sense of mission towards not only the young but the whole extended community of the school – students, staff and parents. The use of the word 'incarnational' is illuminating: it recalls the doctrine of the incarnation, the embodiment of God in Christ, Jesus as 'the body language of God', as Martyn Percy has recently put it – and conveys a sense of the chaplain's responsibility to 'embody' the gospel. The chaplain is also 'an identified Christian': this adds a further layer of meaning to the notion of 'the public face of God' or 'the God person' but avoids any sense that the chaplain is somehow alone as a Christian in the school, an isolated figure crying in the wilderness. A chaplain is both an identified Christian, and the one charged with embodying the faith, being its public representative.

In the following reflection a priest–chaplain who serves in a large, inner-city Church academy but who has no formal teaching programme considers some of the implications of this 'ministry of presence':

> For me, having a 'ministry of presence' is a distinctive gift that a priest brings to their work as a school chaplain. It involves being there for people; my ministry of presence means that I am in the privileged position of holding others' stories – not with an agenda, but as the 'God' person – it is about knowing and being known: caught in a smile, a glance that is exchanged; a meeting of equals as children-of-God.
>
> And if that is true in pastoral encounter – in personal relationship with others – it is just as true institutionally. Ideally the priest doesn't have a function in a school – or at least their 'role' – in terms of the work of their job – is secondary.

It is by being – by being present – that the priest exercises the ministry of the Christ who is incarnate: it is the reality of 'God with us', being for us, that is being lived and witnessed to.

This chaplain's distinctive emphasis on 'knowing and being known', on the centrality of trusted personal relationship in the ministry of chaplaincy, is echoed by a priest–chaplain in the very different context of an independent boarding school, who describes acknowledging and greeting people around the school as part of what his academy colleague calls 'a meeting of equals as children-of-God':

> In walking around the school, I find it very important to try to acknowledge each and every student, even if only with a nod or a wave if I'm in the middle of a conversation with some-body else. I explain why I do this and how encouraging it is to be greeted back . . . I plan to do this without any exceptions at all – and given the chance, to make some sort of comment . . . There is always a risk involved in such encounters – the risk of being ignored or treated as some sort of fool – but the gains far outweigh the losses.

This emphasis on recognition – the 'recognition' of all others without distinction as important, as precious 'children of God' – lies at the core of school chaplaincy. All these chaplains, though exercising very different kinds of chaplaincy in widely differing school contexts, share a vision of what at its heart the identity of a school chaplain encompasses. It is about being present for others, being there with others, being known to and knowing others, all the time being conscious of being the one seen as the 'God person', the one whose presence in some sense 'incarnates' God; makes, that is, the reality of God and the love of God visibly and actually present in the community. The chaplain who spoke of being 'a little Christ' in the school was expressing the same conviction: chaplaincy in school is about being the public face of God, the visible representative of God, both to the young and to those who work and live with them.

Presence and prophecy

Identity and role are closely intertwined for school chaplains. However much they think in terms of their calling to exercise a ministry of presence, the countercultural implications of their identity and being are unavoidable. In Chapter 3, I referred to the dominant educational culture of our time as increasingly focused on output measures, to the potential detriment of spirituality. Two of the chaplains just quoted speak also about the way their presence may be seen as an implicit validation of other, more human and spiritual values than those of the public education system. This suggests that chaplaincy in schools – as perhaps in other contexts too – is a ministry that overtly brings into play spiritual values that may be in tension with those of the institution in which the chaplain ministers. Here, the inner-city chaplain acknowledges that for some of his colleagues the nature of his job seems incomprehensible:

> In people's lack of comprehension of this ministry – in their incredulity that anyone could be paid just to 'be' in a school – a really important lack within our schools is pointed up. Staff in schools can be so headless – running round ineffectively to implement that next initiative from above; so outcome driven – that they forget that their primary vocation is to help young people to become adult humans . . .
>
> The ministry of presence is a reminder of this vocation of human dignity: that in the incarnation God says, 'You are made in my image' and 'I know your story'. And if in a school community human development is undervalued . . . there is a real risk that the spiritual dimension starts to be eclipsed by narrower definitions of educational achievement.

For this chaplain, exercising a ministry of presence may involve calling upon the school community to recover its true ethos, as a place where young people may grow up with a vision of their humanity as given by God, rather than as a place governed simply by measures of educational output.

The nature of institutional life in all its intensity may be something that threatens the very nature of chaplaincy ministry, however. The lay teacher–chaplain highlights the sheer pace and busyness of school life – not least his own life as a teacher – as potentially undermining to a 'ministry of presence':

> Keeping space for this ministry of presence is a continual battle in a busy school. There are always papers, preparations and projects screaming for attention. 'Presence time', together with time spent in prayer, can seem like easy places to win back valuable time, but despite this temptation I am convinced being present is one of the foundations of effective chaplaincy.
>
> In a school environment that seems ever more driven to measure progress and effectiveness, presence ministry is not only countercultural, but I hope, prophetic. In our system young people are so often measured by what they can do. A ministry of presence places people at the heart of the chaplain's, and by implication, God's agenda. It is a visible reminder that to God, who we are, our hearts and our character, is of far greater importance that anything we earn or win.

In their different contexts and school roles, both chaplains sense the potential conflict between the fundamental values of their ministry and the more output-focused values of the system within which their church school operates. This isn't to suggest that a school chaplain is some kind of subversive presence setting out to undermine the work of the school. It is rather that a commitment to the values of gospel-focused and person-centred ministry, a commitment to the spiritual nature of the educational enterprise, may put the chaplain in a position where she or he stands against a dominant educational culture. A ministry of Christian presence implies having a prophetic stance; or, as another chaplain put it, 'waving a flag for sanity', standing for ultimate truths and values, speaking truth – even to power.

'Embedded' chaplaincy – and other models

These chaplains exemplify the most important model of chaplaincy in Church of England schools. 'Embedded' in the school community, they embody the core values of Christian faith and ministry, values that may at times be in tension with the institution. This model derives, I suggested in Chapter 1, from the practice of the nineteenth- and twentieth-century independent schools, where the chaplain was a figure with substantial leadership authority and moral influence within the institution. As chaplaincy developed in the maintained church schools of the post-1944 era, it was this model of the teacher–chaplain that became the norm. However, chaplaincy in the Church's some 200 secondary schools in the new century operates in a variety of diverse ways, reflecting different views of the nature and importance of chaplaincy to a school community and to its spiritual mission and ethos.

Some schools employ a full-time, non-teaching priest–chaplain, as in the case of one of the chaplains just quoted, this model suggesting a strong commitment to a vision of the school as a spiritually focused community. Other schools employ a teacher–chaplain who is a priest – still the predominant model in the independent schools. Others employ a lay teacher–chaplain, as in the case of another chaplain just quoted. Then there are various part-time arrangements that provide for the employment of a non-teaching ordained chaplain for part of the working week, sometimes now as part of a dual role curacy in both a parish and a school. It is hard, though, not to see one- or two-day a week arrangements reflecting a sense that chaplaincy is not high on the school's list of priorities. It raises the obvious questions: How important *is* this ministry? How much does the school really care about the spiritual welfare of its whole community?

Then there is a whole range of voluntary arrangements: perhaps a local parish priest being available for emergency consultation, a local parish or youth worker or volunteer from a local Christian charity, having a regular slot simply visiting in a local school. It is in this latter area that one of the most exciting and potentially challenging developments has taken place in recent years. I described this earlier in Chapter 1 as 'para-chaplaincy', a near but not identical model to the notion of chaplaincy as usually understood. Para-chaplains are characteristically young graduates, trained in church youth work, for whom their – usually evangelically rooted – Christian faith has a powerful motivational force. Often they will work voluntarily, possibly on a 'gap-year' basis and some-times with a view to exploring a possible future life vocation to professional ministry.

There are, however, significant issues raised by para-chaplaincy, which I shall explore later in Chapter 8. For the present I want simply to note that chaplaincy in schools encompasses a very wide range of contexts, individuals and of chaplaincy models. While we do have research data in relation to the practice of embedded chaplains, the motivation, methodology and theology of para-chaplains remain so far unexplored. This makes all the more important the task of developing a clear normative–formal theological understanding of what school chaplaincy really means in the Church of England. To revert to the previous section of this chapter for a moment, it will be clear that in contrast to para-chaplains, whose relationship with schools, staff and pupils is inevitably occasional, an embedded chaplain has the task of 'being present' not only to the individual people he or she meets but also to the institution itself, in a potentially challenging and prophetic role.

Christ and chaplaincy

One of the earliest interviews I conducted as part of the Bloxham/OxCEPT research project remains vividly significant for me. The priest sharing with me her experience and under-standing of chaplaincy in her maintained church school was nearing the end of a two-year counselling course. Reflecting on what she now knew about the 'core conditions' for being an effective counsellor, she described how these conditions – being open to the person and accepting them as they are, receiving non-judgementally what is said and so on – reflected for her the dominical style of ministry, 'how Jesus was with people'.

This is a powerful identification. The ministry of Jesus, I suggested earlier, is the model from which all Christian ministry fundamentally derives, although other models drawn from biblical narrative – for instance the apostolic model – have also been influential. Chaplaincy is, like the ministry of Jesus, a style of ministry to any and all who may be encountered, whatever their identity or relation to the faith community. One chaplain, speaking of his curacy – after which he took up his chaplaincy in an independent day school – said that he had spent much of his time as a parish curate mainly with Christians, which he had found frankly unexciting. In contrast, days spent in school engaging with questioning pupils was stimulating and challenging, more substantially fulfilling.

Another chaplain spoke of the enjoyment of 'being surrounded by lots of non-Christians' in school, something 'not quite so simple as it was in parish life'. Both these chaplains had moved from ministry in what they perceived as the relatively unchallenging world of the local Church community into the very different context of the school. Here, their personal commitment to faith was no longer seen as a means of validation within the community but rather something that invited question. A chaplain's presence in the school community is itself something that opens up the spiritual realm; sheer presence prompts curiosity and question, and the chaplain is therefore inherently an apologist – in the classic sense of needing to defend and to argue for faith, as well as simply representing it.

The chaplain who described her model for ministry as trying to reflect 'how Jesus was with people' went on to say: 'It's back to the Jesus of the Gospels . . . and also about humanity being created in God's image . . . every person is of value and significant.' In this way of thinking, an *imago Dei* theology links directly with a ministerial paradigm derived from the practice of Jesus himself. Another chaplain who had been asked to reflect on her theology of chaplaincy and to present her thinking to fellow chaplains built further on the dominical model. For her, as a priest in an independent day school, Jesus modelled ministry for her in his roles as a rabbi (a spiritual teacher); as a rebel (highlighting his rejection of formal religious custom); and as reconciler (one who would bring people together). For both these chaplains, the gospel imperative for chaplaincy ministry derived directly from the ministry of Jesus himself. We can see this as a key element in the espoused theology of school chaplaincy. This theology impels a chaplain towards an essentially Christ-based ministry, one built on the centrality of the Jesus of the Gospels to ministerial understanding.

Presence and significance

The school chaplain exercising a ministry of presence as an identifiable Christian is carrying out a Christ-derived ministry, even being 'a little Christ' in the school. But what does this presence signify or signpost? Beyond just a physical 'being there', chaplains feel their presence to be indicative, a sign or 'representative symbol', as one chaplain expressed it, of 'spiritual values'. From here it is a short step to the notion of incarnation, of embodiment, already hinted at above. One chaplain spoke of 'modelling what I believe is Christ's way . . . of showing . . . unconditional love . . . it's trying to be incarnational – incarnate in my understanding is God being here . . . I want to signpost God.' Another chaplain spoke similarly of 'being Christian in a particular way . . . the gospel being embodied and lived, living the faith in a different way, that is accessible and embodied and human . . .'

This awareness of the significance of presence is at the heart of the espoused theology of school chaplains. A ministry of presence is seen as a matter both of representing and of 'signposting' or indicating, pointing towards, God, and this in itself can be a way, as one chaplain said, of 'being that presence in a school which encourages, legitimizes people's faith'. Because the chaplain is a visible, representative figure of the Christian faith, embodying its values, he or she supports and enables the faith of others in the community. In a post-Christian age of widespread secularity, it hardly needs emphasizing just how significant it may be for school pupils to have in their community an approachable, adult role model who is visibly and unaffectedly embracing and representing Christian faith. It makes faith a realistic possibility.

This theology of significant or signposting presence, of 'embodying and signifying', seems to lie at the heart of the practice of Church of England school chaplaincy. More than just 'being there' for others in times of pastoral need, it is about being there in a specific way with the deliberate intention of being an embodiment and a signifier of the gospel, incarnating Christ, pointing to God. Intentionality is central. Commenting on the situation of clergy in the current, secular context, Martyn Percy offers an insight which can be applied to school chaplains, both lay and ordained. Clergy, he suggests, 'occupy that strange hinterland between the sacred and the secular, the temporal and the eternal, acting as interpreters and mediators, embodying and signifying faith, hope and love' (2006, p. 188).

In the strange hinterland

In the contemporary school context, a chaplain is occupying precisely that 'hinterland' between sacred and secular, between the world of the Church and the world of contemporary, secular culture inhabited by pupils and staff alike. An embodiment of faith, the chaplain also signposts the central Christian virtues and values of faith, and hope and love. But signposting or indicating is insufficient in itself, just as presence is insufficient. Beyond being able to indicate, the chaplain needs the capacity to mediate between the two worlds of sacred and secular, to interpret one to the other.

The community theologian Ann Morisy has written illuminatingly about this. In her *Journeying Out: A New Approach to Christian Mission* (2004), she highlights the distance between the culture of our time and the inherited understanding of the Church. Given a widespread lack of religious literacy, she suggests, Christian ministers need to adopt an approach that is about working within and yet venturing beyond the limited religious understanding of the unchurched person. This is just the world in which school chaplaincy operates. The task, she says,

> is to work or engage with people to build their confidence in the intimations they have of an enduring reality and the non-material aspects of life . . . a ministry of awakening, helping people to see beyond the daily round of worldly commitment, to awaken in them a sense of their eternal origin and destiny. (p. 152)

The work of chaplaincy, Morisy suggests, is to 'open the conversation of Spirit' with those who do not share the Church's symbolic understandings of faith and who do not have access to the 'high, symbolic repertoire' that links us to the transcendent. Needless to say, this encompasses many or most of the young and those who teach and care for them in church schools.

So a chaplain needs to 'develop the skill of code-switching'; that is, the ability to move from the language and symbolism of faith to the discourse of everyday. The chaplain, suggests Morisy, 'works at the level of the imagination' to help people see beyond the routine and to discover that 'within our ordinary experiences there are rumours of angels and traces of ultimacy' (p. 153). These insights echo strongly the perceptions of chaplains in school: conscious of using a familiar but still incisive term, one chaplain described his task as 'keeping the rumour of God alive'; that is, in the 'strange hinterland' between sacred and secular, a chaplain suggests that there is more to the world and human experience than is at first evident, making talk of God possible.

Outward and visible: a walking sacrament

Metaphorically, a chaplain implicitly 'points us to the skies'. Another way of putting this is to say that chaplaincy in schools is sacramental: the chaplain is an 'outward and visible sign'. This idea was explored by the chaplain–theologian Austin Farrer in a sermon preached in the 1960s at a newly ordained priest's first celebration of the Eucharist. Farrer's address focuses in a highly catholic way on the nature of priesthood. The priest, says, Farrer, has the special responsibility of 'bearing the Sacrament', conveying the living Christ to others. But, he continues, 'the man (sic) who bears the Sacrament is sacramental himself; he is, one might almost say, himself a walking sacrament'. Developing this idea, it is as if Farrer realizes that what is true for the priest must also by extension be true for all Christian people, who in their setting represent Christ: 'None of us can be let off being Christ in our place . . . [God] just puts himself there in our midst; in this bread and in this wine: in this priest: in this Christian man, woman or child' (Loades and MacSwain 2006, pp. 138–41).

So the priest or the chaplain, or the Christian lay person, is a sacramental sign representing Christ, and is even – in Farrer's formulation – a 'walking sacrament'. Such an understanding of ministry seems particularly apposite for chaplaincy. In the school context, a chaplain – whether fully 'embedded' in the community and its life or simply an occasionally visiting 'para-chaplain' – has the huge responsibility and privilege of being Christ to and for others. As the teacher–chaplain I quoted above emphasized: 'For many I will be the only Christian minister who they regularly see and speak to. But only if I make time to be present.' School chaplaincy is about presence with and for the young and their teachers and their parents, pointing beyond to God.

In this chapter I have presented the ministry of school chaplaincy as it is experienced by practitioners, and correlated that experienced perspective with a number of perceptions from 'formal' theology. What emerges is a powerful picture of a distinctive ministry of presence, with chaplains conscious of bearing or even being Christ to those in the community of the school. In the next chapter I shall look at school chaplaincy from the student perspective: how exactly is it seen by the young?

5

'A Sort of Mini-Jesus': How Students Understand Chaplaincy

In the previous chapter I explored one of the core insights of school chaplains about the nature of their ministry: the idea of chaplaincy as a 'ministry of presence'. As part of this exploration I correlated the thinking of practising school chaplains – their espoused theology – with other dimensions of theological thought in order to place school chaplaincy as practitioners experience it in the wider context of the theological understanding of Christian ministry. The further questions this raises are: how is chaplaincy in schools understood by its main client group, school students; and to what extent do they share the perspective of their chaplains? This chapter draws on data from a number of focus groups held as part of the Bloxham/OxCEPT research project described earlier.

Focus groups were held at an independent boarding and day school with a resident chaplain (School A); an inner-city church comprehensive school (now an academy) with a full-time, non-teaching chaplain (School B); a suburban diocesan academy with a part-time, non-teaching chaplain (School C); and a town church comprehensive (now an academy) with a full-time non-teaching chaplain (School D). The chaplains in all these schools were ordained, and the focus groups were arranged with their help. This could have meant that specially chosen, sympathetic students were selected to support the chaplaincy. In the event this wasn't the case. The groups, comprising between eight and 12 students, encompassed male and female, those from several ethnic backgrounds including other-faith students, and both open non-believers and practising Christians. Most were sixth-form students – in one case a group taught an academic subject by the chaplain – though one group was made up of Year 9 students, at that point the most senior pupils in the (then) developing suburban academy. The fundamental question explored in the group discussions was: 'What value, if any, is added to the life of your school by chaplaincy?' Student responses were fascinating: it is clear that school students understand and respond to chaplaincy in terms their chaplains would find familiar.

A recognized and challenging presence

It was while exploring with the focus group in School C the various tasks a chaplain undertakes that the question of the chaplain's identity surfaced. One student objected to my line of questioning: 'But it's not his tasks, it's his "-ness", who he is, his being,' she said. This idea of the essence (the '-ness') of chaplaincy residing in the chaplain's identity or being as a person rather than in the functions he or she performs quite startlingly recalls the perceptions of chaplains themselves about being preceding function, the significance of their 'ministry of presence'. The student who said this could almost have been echoing catholic thinking about the sociological and ontological dimensions of priesthood and the primacy of the ontological. Later in the conversation the same student also articulated something very close to the idea of the chaplain quoted in the previous chapter who said, 'ultimately I'm a little Christ here'. Reflecting on the non-teaching role of her chaplain, she said: 'I think the fact that he's not a teacher makes him more approachable'; and then went on: 'He's like a scaled-down version of Jesus, a kind of mini-Jesus.'

This is a powerful insight. We can't assume that every student in a church school with a chaplain would express this

view; but for this student – and we might hope for others too –
the core theological insight of the chaplain being a personal
Christ-representative, an *alter Christus*, is telling. Similarly telling is the view students took on their chaplain as a role model.
At School D one student spoke about the importance of 'being
comfortable with yourself and what you believe' and having faith
in oneself rather than just in a religion. She went on, however,
to say that 'a really good, positive role model' was helpful for
students, and identified this as one aspect of chaplaincy: 'I think
[the chaplain] is a positive role model . . . it makes us aspire to
be good people and want to help the community.' It seems that
even where the chaplain's faith may not be shared, her or his
modelling of Christian behaviour can be influential. But much
appears to depend upon the chaplain's approachability, as highlighted by the student quoted just above. In all the focus groups,
students spoke favourably of the chaplain's being available and
approachable; and in School D a student, asked to identify what
she saw as the heart of someone being 'chaplain material', as she
put it, responded: 'being approachable is the key to it'.

This is something in which a chaplain might be distinctly different from the other members of the school staff; and students
were able to identify clearly the different positions of chaplain
and teacher within the school. Even where the chaplain was
also a teacher, that was just a matter, as one student put it, of
'different hats'. What distinguished the chaplain was that he
or she was open to others, approachable and able to deal with
confidential issues – something it might be difficult to assume a
hard-pressed teacher, focused on getting students good grades
in examinations, would be. Students also seemed to recognize
that the chaplain represented a set of values and priorities that
might conflict with those of the educational world, echoing the
perceptions of chaplains quoted in the previous chapter who
saw themselves as at least potentially at odds with the educational culture of the present time.

For one student in School D, this was a key issue. 'Schools
aren't just for teaching, they're also to develop people as part

of the community and that's the aspect where [chaplains] earn their pay, developing students.' Another student expanded this idea:

> I think it defines the school; it would be just another school if we didn't have a chaplaincy . . . I think that this school tries to create rounded individuals, it's not just looking for the grades . . . it's not just focused on getting the grades, it's actually about building a person.

This student's insight, that chaplaincy is linked with 'building a person', points clearly to the formative effect of school ethos, and resonates strongly with the pastoral imperative towards human flourishing and spiritual development. The values a chaplain embodies and represents, suggests the student, are central to the personal development which schools in the Christian tradition are concerned to foster.

The chaplain becomes, in this view, almost an exponent – even a guarantor – of a set of values rooted in faith, someone 'embedded' within the world of education (to take Paul Ballard's description – see page 50) but committed to seeing beyond it, and reflecting on it in the light of faith. Students seemed to perceive quite clearly that there is at least a potential institutional tension in church schools between the values of a faith-based focus on the person, and the current public emphasis on the acquisition of educational credentials through achieving examination success, an overwhelming concern with outcome measures, or 'grades'. On the one hand stands a spiritual value system based on the uniqueness of the individual as a child of God, on fostering their development towards maturity, 'to the measure of the full stature of Christ' (Eph. 4.13). On the other is an economically derived and competitively driven concern with 'maximizing student outcomes'. School chaplaincy seems to be valued by these students as an expression of the values of 'building a person': a chaplain brings a recognized – and challenging – presence to the school.

A distinctive and intermediary role

One student perspective, then, sees the school chaplain as to some extent set apart from the wider, results-driven culture of education, representing the best efforts of the church school to 'create rounded individuals'. The perception that the chaplain has a distinctive role within the institution of the school, significantly different from that of the ordinary teacher, also seems to be one widely shared among students. At School A, a boarding community, there appeared to be a particular dimension to this. In this school, whose Christian identity is proclaimed through the centrality of its magnificent school chapel, the chaplain was seen by students as 'a similar figure to the headmaster' – similar in status though different in presence.

Especially valued by students was this chaplain's wide involvement in all aspects of school life: 'he involves himself in everything, sport, music, lunchtime concerts', commented one student. And this involvement related to the chaplain's approachability: 'being around' was seen as a prerequisite for his being approached by students as a potential ally in their cause – as a trusted figure in the school he could be relied on to represent the interests and opinions of students to the leadership team, and to achieve positive outcomes for the student body. To this extent a school chaplain can be a kind of intermediary figure. Not constrained or limited by – in this case – a high-profile role in liturgical leadership, remaining as far as students are concerned 'much more approachable', he can also be a trusted advocate for the student community, and also for individual students. This implies that a chaplain has a measure of independence in relation to the power structures of the school, a position as a trusted go-between.

Our research indicated that while a very few school chaplains – just 6 per cent of respondents – do have a place in the formal leadership team of the school, the overwhelming majority do not. Even where a chaplain is officially a member of the school leadership team, that role may be more about advice and comment in support of the team's work than about actual decision-making. The perception that clergy work in 'that strange hinterland between the sacred and the secular, the temporal and the eternal, acting as interpreters and mediators' (Percy 2006) seems especially relevant. A school chaplain, students suggest, may helpfully play the role of both mediator and interpreter in the complex power world of the boarding school, and in the more usual context of the day school too. As one student in School A commented: 'Between students and teachers there's a big divide, and he kind of stands in the middle ground.' While for a student in School B, 'the chaplain is there to be a link . . . a kind of bridge from school to faith'.

Representing religion, leading spirituality

Linking the worlds of school and faith, a school chaplain is inevitably seen as 'representing religion'. Asked about the most important element in a chaplain's job, some students argued for this being the leading of public worship while others argued for the pastoral role – highlighting what chaplains themselves see as two core functions. As far as worship is concerned, one student noted the contrast between the 'very kind of graded and black and white' world of school learning, and the altogether different world of readings and prayers in school assembly, a context for 'something spiritual which can't necessarily be defined'. This aspect of the chaplain's role – opening up the spiritual realm through prayer and worship – links also for students with the public and representative aspect of chaplaincy. One student put it like this: the chaplain 'heads the . . . Christian principles the school holds'.

Reflecting further on this, and on what happens if a church school has no chaplain, students emphasized the self-evident link, as it seemed to them, between chaplaincy and church schools. 'We define ourselves as a Church of England school,' said one School B student, adding: 'To take away that religious head figure . . . would degrade the school, almost.' Asked what difference losing a chaplain might make, another student argued that 'the chaplain adds value to the school', going on to say that 'having a chaplain provides a kind of spiritual education'. Admitting that not all students would lament the loss of a chaplain, however, another student added: 'You are taking away something which maybe not all of the students want, but the majority of students want and are happy to see.'

Students appear to value highly the personal leadership of the spiritual dimension of education a chaplain provides, but they also realize that 'though one person has the job . . . it's not just a solo effort, his message is throughout the school'. Without a chaplain a school would be different, lacking spiritual leadership and a spiritual reference point for staff. It could even, said a student in School B, mean this: 'To take away a religious leader from the school is to take away the religious ethos.' This recognition of the central public and leadership aspect of chaplaincy ministry in schools is hugely significant. It seems that while the Church of England has as yet no policy on school chaplaincy – and indeed as we saw in Chapter 3 appears to have sidelined chaplaincy in its official reports on church-based education – school students have a clear understanding of what chaplaincy in a school signifies. For these students, the ethos of a church school is somehow embodied in its chaplain, who is committed to exemplifying and championing the very values on which the school's foundation rests. The chaplain is a guarantor of the school's Christian identity.

This raises the question of the role and responsibility of heads and governing bodies in safeguarding the Christian character of a church school. It is surely right to see the governors of a school – especially when the school operates as a Trust, and they are Trustees – as those given the task of safeguarding the ongoing, foundation identity of the school, in partnership with the current head and leadership team. While heads and their leadership colleagues are temporary, and are usually appointees of the governing body, it is the permanent governing body itself which has to define, support and maintain what that ongoing identity should be, and how it should be expressed in the life of the school and experienced by students. While most students will inevitably see the head as the leader of the educational life of the school, the one who sets the overall boundaries and creates the rules and procedures, it is arguably the chaplain who leads the school's spiritual life, and who expresses the school's Christian identity and vision through worship and pastoral care, and through embodying, representing and upholding the values of the school's foundation. One student ended up searching for words on this issue:

> [We] wouldn't be the same school without a Church representative . . . . It's in the name . . . a Church of England school without anyone to lead religion within it is sort of just . . . you remove how the school started out.

In this student perspective, chaplaincy is a vital element in the continuing identity of a church school, a guarantor of enduring values.

The school chaplain and pastoral care

I argued in Chapter 1 that at the heart of mission and ministry is the giving of pastoral care: the disinterested provision of caring support to all in need, simply because of who they are as children of God, with the aim of supporting their flourishing as human beings. Students clearly identified the pastoral role as central to school chaplaincy, although discussion brought out some uncertainties in student understanding of what counts as 'pastoral' – a question I shall consider further in Chapter 6. But the basic certainty that chaplains offer pastoral care was clear to students. Asked to define the most important thing a chaplain does, one School A student simply said 'care', as if that word alone sufficed. Another expressed the point like this: 'He's there for the students'; and this response captured a sense almost of student ownership of the chaplain, someone who was there for them in a way different from teachers, someone who would put them first: 'He's just like someone to bridge the gap pastorally and just to be there for everyone.'

This view was amplified by a student in School B. 'His purpose as a chaplain here is to . . . guide people through their religious journeys, their spiritual journeys,' he said. Another added, 'As a religious figure in the school he's there to offer spiritual advice . . . His name is Father [name], and he is basically like a father to the students.' This perception of the personal support offered by the chaplain as focused on the spiritual and religious realms but delivered distinctively in a caring, even paternal way is refreshing – and school chaplains employ a variety of titles, or indeed none, and 'Father' is only one. It gives a degree of precision to the term 'care' and makes clear that in these students' understanding 'pastoral care' does not descend to the pointless level described by Stephen Pattison as 'a minor and trivial activity of personal niceness to people without purpose, skill or theological significance' (2008, p. 9). For students, a chaplain's 'care' really counts, as the care of a parent or friend does: it isn't an expression of bland benignity.

And for students in School B the chaplain's pastoral care related clearly to the spiritual dimension. One student explained: 'If it was to do with their studies, they would go to their teachers, if it was their social life they'll go to their friends, if it was their home life they'll go to their parents or siblings.' While this categorization may be simplistic, it does make clear the view that the chaplain is there for matters relating to faith. A School B student commented: 'No matter if you're a Christian or atheist or agnostic or Muslim it doesn't matter with him – you can go to him and talk to him about faith.' In School A, a student contrasted the outlook of 'normal' teachers with what the chaplain represented. Summing up what a chaplain added to school life he said simply:

I think it's care, because when you have normal teachers you don't know if they're there for you or for their pay cheque . . . it's like when [the chaplain] says hello to you it's more because he wants to rather than because of the money in his pocket.

While this comment may cast a sad light on the financially rooted thinking of some independent school students, it is revealing: the chaplain clearly stands for and represents a distinct and different set of values.

But there might well be things that, in the understanding of students, come outside the chaplain's pastoral remit, his or her caring concern. Reflecting on the separate roles of the resident chaplain and the visiting school counsellor, students at School A thought that their female counsellor would be preferred 'if it was like a female problem' or 'something psychological'; whereas for social or interpersonal matters such as bullying they would go to their chaplain. 'That can be something very personal you wouldn't discuss with teachers,' said one student; 'It does depend what the problem is.' Another student added: 'And it does depend on who you are.' For this last student, who would not go to the counsellor simply because she didn't like her, conversations with the chaplain were also limited. A day student, she contrasted her own situation – able to go home and share problems and concerns with her family – with that of boarding students, for whom a resident chaplain was identified with them in a way a visiting or 'separate' counsellor could not be.

In summary, student perceptions of chaplaincy seem to highlight a caring role, probably focused on the spiritual dimension and matters of faith but having an important reach into the area of the 'personal', an area 'ordinary teachers' might not be interested in or appropriate to consult about. Pastoral care therefore seems for students at the forefront of a chaplain's role; but this perception may be as unilluminating as it is obvious. What actually counts as pastoral care? How does the school itself, in which there is a whole and complex 'pastoral system', understand the pastoral role of chaplaincy in relation to that system? And how does the role of chaplain interact with that of school counsellor? These are key questions to be explored in the next chapter. They force us to examine what we understand by the mission of the Church and to try to be clear about the nature not just of chaplaincy but also of ministry more generally.

Assemblies, liturgy and worship

In all the schools represented by this sample of students, as we might assume in all church schools, assemblies and worship have a significant place. How do school students understand the chaplain's role in relation to this prominent aspect of their school's life? In School A, whose premises could be seen as a kind of public architectural statement of the significance of Christian faith, students naturally associated their chaplain with the chapel and the services held there. To these students it was self-evident that a chaplain was an absolutely necessary member of the school staff: the school 'wouldn't work' without a chaplain, 'because the chapel is such a part of life here . . . the chapel is really, really important'. Here, the weekly corporate Eucharist, which brings together the whole school community of staff and students, is a regular celebration of the school's identity and nature, something that binds together the whole community even where an individual may not personally embrace the faith.

Other schools have different ways of celebrating their church identity. In School B the chaplain's work in preparing the daily prayers and reflections in common use across the school is seen as a particular expression of his role. This church school with a multi-ethnic, multi-faith make-up remains specifically Christian, one student suggested, through the commonality of 'the readings and the prayers' in assemblies. At the same time, though, a Muslim student recognized that the chaplain's role extended to supporting 'different religious groups' and that the chaplain would 'try to give them the help they need'. Referring to informal 'reflective circles' arranged by the chaplain, and to Bible study groups, the same student spoke of the human commonality of the school's ethos. Participating in such groups, he said, was more about 'your opinion as a human being than as someone from a different faith group'. At School D, one student expressed this inclusive vision of chaplaincy strongly:

> The chaplain . . . has the role no matter what the religion to care for the spiritual needs of whatever people, no matter what the spirituality, Islam or any other religion.

This student's inclusive vision says something profound about the nature of Christian community and the ethos of the church school. In Chapter 3, I suggested that school ethos was a 'prime agent of religious socialization . . . an introduction to the way of faith'. In this student's perception, chaplaincy expresses the inclusive nature of the school community: it is a ministry for all without distinction. Similarly, the school ethos this evokes is one of inclusion, in which each member of the community is valued whatever their spiritual or religious stance. Paul Avis has suggested that by 'building salutary forms of community the Church is creating the climate of moral values, actualized in human relations, within which people find it possible to believe' (2003, p. 184). It is in the inclusive, community ethos of the church school that all students can experience a sense of unconditional belonging, whether or not they share the school's faith stance. Belonging will encourage a shared way of behaving – a way of being human – and the question of believing is a later one. The school's ethos, however, makes the possibility of belief clear: and the chaplain incarnates that possibility for others of both faith and non-faith backgrounds.

From the student perspective it is possible for both a Christian corporate identity and a recognition and celebration of difference to be effectively maintained in a single school. The church school doesn't need to be or be seen as a place of forced conformity. What is required is a chaplaincy aware of and adaptive to the needs of the school's different internal constituencies. Common worship in both the schools just referred to appears not to be about the imposition of religious conformity but rather to be a context for the fostering of open thought, reflection and spirituality in the light of Christian faith. Non-Christian students – both of avowed atheist and other-faith loyalties – appeared happy in both schools to respect and yet not adhere personally to the school's corporate Christian commitment. The school's official faith might be compared to a state's established religion: the system of thought and belief publicly authorized yet remaining wholly non-compulsory for individual members of the community (see Williams 2014).

But it would be wrong to assume that all students blithely accepted the school's official faith. In School D another, more critical perspective emerged. Though one student said that the most important thing the chaplain did was to 'take the Eucharists', and other students noted that she was 'passionate' about worship, and 'expert' in leading it, reservations surfaced. One student referred to 'the scepticism that surrounds assemblies', going on to say:

> That's when you get the most religious input, when you get assemblies and everyone says 'Oh no, it's assembly, we don't want to believe that' . . . There are poignant meanings in what [the chaplain] says, but you sometimes lose those because of the scepticism.

This response can – perhaps paradoxically – be seen as encouraging for chaplaincy. Any sense that students are forearmed against any kind of religious expression could be worrying, but for them to approach faith claims in a critical and questioning spirit can be seen as evidence of growth in both the intellectual and spiritual spheres.

For students are going through a stage of rapid personal development in their secondary years, and perhaps especially in the sixth form. Values are being sought and defined, a whole approach to living being put in place. One A-level student in School B illustrates this. Following the focus group session, this student described privately the way she had been at one point a keen member of the school's Christian group but had later dissociated herself from it. A student of philosophy, theology and ethics, she had found herself questioning her faith, and following a weekend away with the group had found herself now so alienated by their approach that she no longer wanted to 'assign herself' as a Christian. At this point she had sought the advice of the chaplain who, she said, had helped her through discussion during a period in which she questioned and then discarded her earlier, simpler faith. Questioning – a natural activity for sixth-formers – can lead, in Fowler's terms, towards the development of a more mature and 'individuative-reflective' faith (Fowler 1981). Chaplains may find student scepticism a good basis for discussion and faith development.

Chaplaincy, representation and relationship

The student perceptions I have recounted are telling; they offer insights that deserve to be taken seriously by anyone concerned with how the young relate and respond to the Christian faith. They demonstrate too that a school chaplain's ministry may be clearly understood within the school community, its inner nature identified and its wider significance grasped. While, for instance, students might not be able to employ the theological language of 'a ministry of presence', there is every indication that they recognize the chaplain as a person whose ministry is one in which simply 'being there' for others is significant. Students appear alert to the values the chaplaincy represents and that may exist in a relationship of some tension with the educational objectives of the school where these focus too exclusively on 'grades' and leave out a concern for personal growth or formation as a person.

Simply, students can 'read' chaplaincy. They seem to understand clearly both what it implicitly stands for (a way of valuing human beings summed up in the word 'care') and what is explicitly expressed in the worship (the public readings, prayers and eucharistic actions) of the school community. The meaning of a school chaplain's pastoral and liturgical ministry is grasped by students. More than this, however, there seems to be among students a recognition of the significance of the chaplain's very being: this person is someone who represents and signifies faith, who signposts its values and can even be seen as a kind of embodiment of Christ – 'a mini-Jesus'. The theological insights of students into the nature of school chaplaincy parallel closely the stance of school chaplains themselves: here is a ministry whose vocational meaning is understood both by those called to serve and those to whom they offer service.

One vital factor in this not specifically discussed so far is the quality of the relationship between chaplain and students. It would have seemed inappropriate and intrusive to have questioned students directly about how well they got on personally with their chaplain, but what emerged in all the focus groups was a genuine degree of respect for the chaplain as a person. In an age where 'being oneself' and 'being true to oneself' is a key value for the young, any whiff of hypocrisy is rapidly sensed by students. For these students, their chaplains were people of genuineness and authenticity, without pretence or subterfuge. One student at School A described his chaplain like this: 'He's been a foil, philosophical, thought-provoking both religious and personal, a person you can talk to.' Describing her chaplain's response to the sudden death of a pupil in the year group, a School D student said: 'There was nobody else I think who could have dealt with that. She always stayed professional but she did it all in the right way . . . that's the time when I've been most touched by her work.' Whether in personal conversation or in the public response to events, school chaplaincy seems for students to be about human genuineness, about a professional role sensitively and feelingly exercised.

Though the research base of this chapter is small – just a few focus group discussions – I believe that it offers clear and strong evidence that embedded chaplaincy in church schools works, that it is a ministry understood and respected by its student client-group. The only other published evidence on student response to chaplaincy comes from a rather different context in Irish schools, but interestingly offers similar conclusions. Siobhan Murphy's work reflects the outcomes of the

Bloxham/OxCEPT research; she notes 'the depth of respect and genuine feeling exhibited by pupils towards their chaplain', and goes on to argue that 'the findings indicate that the chaplain may be a pivotal force in the personal development of pupils' (2004, p. 185). The chaplains studied in the research project were clearly committed to the personal development of students, and it is to their pastoral role, in which this priority is foremost, that I shall turn in the next chapter.

6

Being with People:
Christian Pastoral Care in
the School Context

Student perceptions of school chaplaincy, as we have seen, highlight the chaplain's pastoral care as a central aspect of his or her work. 'It's care', said one student, asked to sum up what chaplaincy is about. But 'care' and 'pastoral care' are terms that need some clarification, perhaps especially in the professional world of education. In this chapter I shall outline an approach to pastoral care in the context of school chaplaincy that specifically incorporates the spiritual dimension, and consider the potential confusion between 'educational' pastoral care and a chaplain's pastoral care, in the process looking at the relationship between pastoral care and counselling in schools. I shall try to identify some of the key pastoral issues for school students in our current context, and suggest ways in which chaplaincy may support students negotiating these issues.

Pastoral care: at the heart of mission

It became clear from the in-depth interviews I conducted with school chaplains as part of the Bloxham/OxCEPT research project that two dimensions of their role – the pastoral and the liturgical – were uppermost in their minds, a conclusion endorsed by our subsequent online survey. But the pastoral dimension emerged as the one chaplains put ahead of others –

even in those contexts where liturgy played a central part in the school's life. A chaplain from the catholic tradition, asked to say whether liturgy or pastoral care came first for him, said: 'It must be being with people in the end.' Another chaplain, from the evangelical tradition, spoke of the centrality for him of the image of the pastor:

> That is exactly how I see my role, it's to know my sheep by name and to seek those who are lost . . . it's about finding those who are lost and helping them to feel found, to be found, to heal.

Across the ecclesial spectrum, it seems, school chaplains prioritize the pastoral: just as students identify its centrality.

But how does this priority for pastoral care relate to the Church's mission? Stephen Pattison, whose liberation-based understanding of pastoral care I introduced in Chapter 1, contrasts two understandings of pastoral care, which we could label 'weak' and 'strong'. The weak understanding consists in effect of nothing much more than being nice to people – not in itself a bad thing, but in Pattison's description: 'a minor and trivial activity of personal niceness to people without purpose, skill or theological significance'. If chaplaincy in schools were simply about dispensing personal niceness, it would, as Pattison insists, be pretty pointless. But the 'strong' understanding of pastoral care, an activity concerned with our human well-being and relationship with God, has profound missional seriousness; it is 'attending to and nurturing God's world, and all that is in it, for God's sake' (Pattison 2008, p. 9); an activity whose functions are 'healing, sustaining, reconciling, guiding and nurturing' (Pattison 1997, p. 14). This is ministry in the pattern of Jesus.

A school chaplain's pastoral care, in this 'strong' sense, comes from the heart of the gospel: it responds to the dominical story of the lost sheep referenced by the chaplain just quoted, and to Jesus' command, 'feed my sheep' (John 21.17). It is a response, also, to the profound biblical tradition of respect for the created

84

order: nothing and no one should be left uncared for, untended, unnurtured. God's world is precious, to be cared for, as are all the people – children of God – in it. The chaplain quoted just above went on to say:

> My work is about growing souls, being involved in watching people grow and learn . . . being involved in the nurture, growth, development and shape of young people's lives.

This is an espoused theology of school chaplaincy in which pastoral care is a distinctively spiritual activity, concerned with nurturing the whole person. It lies at the very heart of mission. For as Paul Avis has argued: 'The cutting edge of mission is not words. Without living proof that we love and care, words will fall on deaf ears . . . Pastoral care stands in the vanguard of mission' (2003, p. 180). This emphasis rightly sees pastoral care as enacting the gospel, taking the example of Jesus in healing and ministering, and following it. It is, as the practical theologian David Lyall argues, care for the totality of the person in the light of God (2001).

Lyall presents a picture of pastoral care very close to that offered by the chaplain whose description of his work I have just quoted; and given the range of definitions of 'pastoral care' as understood by educational and counselling professionals in their spheres, it is imperative for school chaplains to embrace an understanding that is genuinely drawn from the gospel. This, says Lyall, is a matter of relating the Christian story and the rich tradition of the Church to pastoral practice. He writes: 'Pastors must exercise ministry in the tension between the story of the Christian community and its tradition and the particularity of individual life stories' (2001, p. 61). What the heart of the Christian story – the Incarnation – essentially provides, he suggests, is a vision of God as one who identifies with and enters into the suffering of men and women. Thus, underlying all pastoral ministry is the *agape*, the love of God; and there is nothing so profoundly missional as good pastoral care: 'This is the place where the gospel becomes an embodied response to human need and grace becomes incarnate' (p. 107).

Mission and pastoral care have sometimes been presented as alternative priorities (Pattison 2008); but writing about the ministry and mission of the Church of England in his *Church Drawing Near: Spirituality and Mission in a Post-Christian Culture*, Avis significantly titles his final chapter 'The Primacy of the Pastoral' (2003). His thinking about the nature of pastoral care echoes Pattison's liberationist stance; his argument is that the Church only vindicates its place in society when it is seen to be committed to the healing of human identity and the nurturing of human wholeness – pastoral care, in brief. The provision of chaplaincy in church schools, offering the Church's pastoral care through its lay or ordained ministers to the growing and developing younger generation – 'nurturing wholeness' – is a powerful sign of the Church's commitment to the young, not as potential, future, paid-up church members, but simply as the people they are and are becoming, 'for God's sake'. Equally, not to offer this kind of pastoral care to the young is to declare something very different.

'Pastoral care' as an educational practice

Pastoral care, however, isn't a theological term owned by the Church; it also has a developed educational meaning in the context of English schools, and this is a possible source of confusion. A brief glance at the origins of pastoral care as a distinctive feature of English educational practice will elucidate this. It can be traced to the nineteenth-century independent schools and the house system, in which the house master assumed day-to-day responsibility for the general well-being of students living with him and his family. This period also saw the appointment of school chaplains, as earlier indicated: ordained ministers who would lead daily and weekly worship, teach, and provide moral instruction and spiritual leadership for the student body. So two strands of 'pastoral care' developed: the general well-being of students was the concern of the housemaster; spiritual and moral welfare were for the chaplain.

From 1944 onwards many secondary schools adopted house systems, and it was in the context of houses – usually vertical, multi-age slices through the school – that educational pastoral care was offered, a general concern for the educational and personal well-being of the pupil, without any specifically spiritual dimension. The wholesale reform of the state schools in the 1970s, bringing a near universal comprehensive system, saw a further development of pastoral care, now deemed an essential aspect of any school's organization. In the new comprehensives, heads of house or heads of year – where the pastoral system was based on horizontal year groups – were appointed to support and manage student behaviour, with teams of form tutors, who while they might not themselves teach the students in their group, were regarded as having general oversight of their well-being.

How exactly does a chaplain fit into this picture, in either the independent or maintained church school context? This remains an unresolved and potentially conflict-laden issue. In independent church schools tensions can emerge between house staff and chaplains over the question: 'Whose problem is this and who deals with it?' Similarly in the church-maintained school, a chaplain's role and responsibility may be uncertainly defined in relation to house or year systems. What seems essential – though as yet far from universal – is a clear pastoral referral system that takes full account of the distinctive role of a chaplain. Some schools already have regular 'pastoral' co-ordination meetings in which both chaplain, school counsellor and any medical staff meet with house or year pastoral staff under the chairmanship of a school leadership team member. In some schools the chaplain may for management purposes be accountable to a pastoral deputy head or work within a student services team – a pattern now widely adopted in colleges and universities. In other schools chaplains may – simply because of poor management structures or staff relationships – be among the last to learn of bereavements, relationship breakdowns in students' families or other critical events affecting students' lives.

The potential confusions of understanding about what is meant by 'pastoral care' in a school with a chaplaincy are legion. What seems crucial is for both chaplain and school to have a clear grasp of what is particular, and special, about 'pastoral care' in the mission of the Church and in the work of the chaplain. As one chaplain put it, a key question is: 'how my role overlaps and fits in with other pastoral roles in the school'. Neither a bland being nice to people nor a benevolent concern with the student as a kind of educational add-on, true pastoral care as offered by chaplains needs to be seen as the front line of the mission of the Church: 'attending to and nurturing' the person created in the image of God 'for God's sake'.

Pastoral care in practice: 'unconditional care'

For the school chaplain, pastoral care in practice is at an every-day level about the offer of distinctively spiritual care for the individual person as a child of God. One chaplain describes his task as 'offering gentle, unconditional care for the whole school community'. But some church schools now have both chaplains and school counsellors, as well as other pastoral staff, and it is important to try to be clear about what these roles may have in common and what differentiates them. Chaplains have a sense that all personal issues are in some sense spiritual – that is, that the personal life has a spiritual dimension for everyone, where we understand 'the spiritual' to involve our relationship with ourselves, with others, with the transcendent, with God. To this extent it is arguable that there is no issue that might be taken to a counsellor that could not be equally taken to a chaplain.

This has important, interpersonal implications. One of the School A students quoted in the previous chapter simply didn't like her school counsellor and therefore would not consult her. Others in the group were clear that they would consult the counsellor about some things but definitely not others. Equally, some students might simply 'not like' their chaplain, and this significant interpersonal dimension is a reminder that one of the necessary qualities for school chaplaincy is an ability to relate interpersonally and significantly with all kinds of student and with the full range of members of the school's adult community, to be 'all things to all people'. One chaplain in his independent day school describes his pastoral work in this way: 'A big part of my role is about . . . building up lots of little relationships and sometimes big relationships'; and it is likely that the big relationships develop from the smaller ones. The importance of this fundamental aspect of school chaplaincy – being in the community as a person who relates easily and naturally with others of all kinds – cannot be overestimated: good interpersonal relationships and pastoral effectiveness seem interdependent.

'Others of all kinds' are likely to include students who are a real problem for teachers. One lay chaplain describes his work in a church academy as often focused on the difficult or socially excluded student, the one whose personal issues of background or upbringing are acted out in uncooperative behaviour or negative attitudes. When such a student has been excluded from class or is in danger of exclusion from school as a consequence of 'acting out' behaviour, it is the chaplain who represents the school's last 'pastoral' resort, the one who will pick up the pieces others can't handle. Here the chaplain has a dual function: he plays a role in the school's pastoral system, while also being engaged pastorally with the student at a personal level, probably seeking to help the student to understand the sources of his or her own behaviour, 'nurturing wholeness'. For another chaplain, her work with 'the disaffected' has real personal impact: she relates how the eventual exclusion from school of a difficult student she had worked with left her with 'a great sense of bereavement'.

Pastoral care in practice: personal counselling

What distinguishes counselling from pastoral care? A school counsellor will probably have been trained in counselling and psychotherapeutic techniques; will be accredited through the British Association for Counselling and Psychotherapy (BACP) and will practise in line with the BACP ethical framework (see British Association for Counselling and Psychotherapy 2014). The school chaplain will not necessarily have had any such background. The BACP ethical framework sets high professional standards. In addition to setting out the values implicit in counselling, and describing the personal moral qualities required of a practitioner, such as empathy, sincerity, integrity, resilience, respect and humility, it offers guidance on good practice and sets out key ethical principles: being trustworthy; autonomy (respect for the client's right to be self-governing); beneficence (commitment to promoting the client's well-being); non-maleficence (a commitment to avoiding harm to the client); justice (the fair and impartial treatment of all clients); and self-respect (fostering the practitioner's self-knowledge and care for self).

Though the school chaplain may have no formal counselling qualification, the BACP ethical framework could well be taken as a guide for his or her own work with individual students and staff. Arguably, school chaplains – like one quoted earlier (see page 60) – who have themselves undertaken BACP counselling training may well be in a better position to offer personal support for students. Despite what critics have seen as the 'value-free' nature of person-centred counselling approaches, BACP offers an ethically serious stance that is in fact in key respects echoed by the chaplains I interviewed for the research project. One, for instance, referred to Paul Tillich's saying 'the first duty of love is to listen', going on to describe her own experience of intent listening: 'when someone is in a state of affliction . . . you really do listen with such compassion and imagination to what the other is going through'. The same chaplain describes how at the end of a pastoral session, a student had asked her: 'Have I really been talking to you for an hour?'

This kind of focused attentiveness – rooted in empathy, characterized by compassion and imagination – can be seen as the basis of all helpful and effective counselling, whether offered by a counsellor or chaplain. But the school chaplain does offer 'added value'. The chaplain just quoted, for instance, refers to her faith perspective providing the trust and hope that students will be enabled to 'work things out for themselves'; and she sees this as 'working within some sort of dimension of God's love and Spirit'. Another chaplain speaks of:

> Trying to be aware of God's presence in all the conversations I have . . . showing God's love and concern even if I don't actually speak those words . . . I suppose what I'm always trying to do is to say, 'This is where God is . . . how can we become more aware of God's presence around us in everyday life?'

These chaplains are consciously undertaking their pastoral work in the light not only of the professional requirements for good counselling practice but also of the spiritual context of human relationships: all our meetings with others take place in the presence of God. Hence pastoral counselling can be seen as part of the work of God. For the chaplain, the person seeking counsel – student or staff member, parent or governor – is above all a unique and precious child of God, whom God wants to flourish as a full, human person. The spiritual dimension is the heart of the matter: it may be signalled to the other person by the lighting of a candle; by the setting aside of a few moments for silent reflection; by the sheer focus of the chaplain's listening; by the saying of a prayer. The chaplain is working not simply with a person-focused approach but also within the long Christian tradition of spiritual care, where the pastor is charged with being a 'physician of souls' (Purves 2001).

This is above all about the chaplain's own individual faith, her or his own personal authenticity. One chaplain says:

> We are all who we are . . . I try to give of myself because I don't feel there's anything else to give, I have to be who I am in it because that's the thing that works, and the students know, they know what comes authentically from a teacher and a priest.

A chaplain in school is under the quizzical scrutiny of a shrewdly observant student community, and the young are adept at spotting insincerity, any lack of genuineness or profundity. A chaplain has first to be who she or he actually is, a person of faith, someone who recognizes the significance of their perceived role as a 'mini-Jesus', and who is able to respond to students and staff from the depth of his or her spiritual being, the place of deepest authenticity. It is from this place that genuine compassion and empathy flow, and will be recognized by 'the other': *cor ad cor loquitur* – heart speaks to heart, in a dialogue where God is the animating presence. As one chaplain says: 'I think prayer happens sometimes in the silence and in the conversation.'

Pastoral care in practice: personal issues

A prayerful ministry of pastoral care can be healing and sustaining – and there is no shortage of need for this in the present age of uncertainty and anxiety. A key feature of our times, as we saw earlier, is what Charles Taylor calls 'the turn to the subjective', and a consequent focus on personal choice and responsibility. Normal teenage concerns about identity and ambition, relationships with others, emerging sexuality and the meaning of life continue to predominate, but now without the structures of expected behaviour familiar to earlier generations. This means that chaplains find themselves inhabiting a tradition of teaching about personal conduct – what is expected of Christian, moral or good behaviour – when many young people who may come for counsel do not have a similar background of ethical responsibility. Put simply, the dilemma looks like this: given traditional Christian ideals for living – for instance simplicity of life, active concern for the other, personal chastity – how best can school chaplains support students growing up in a world that assumes the need for massive consumption of consumer goods, self-focused thinking and largely unrestrained sexual expression?

Chaplains need careful, delicate poise: both understanding the pressures of the culture, and honouring the ideals of conduct Christian faith has traditionally promoted. This means that as a pastoral counsellor the chaplain works in a subtly different way from the school counsellor, whose commitment will simply be to the well-being of the client, irrespective of traditional faith-based ideals of behaviour. While the chaplain will share that commitment to the student's well-being, she or he will also seek to bring to bear on the understanding of 'well-being' the values of the gospel. Chaplaincy in schools is necessarily about inhabiting both the world of the young and the world of ongoing Christian values; and one task of the church school – and of school chaplains – is to help the young negotiate the complex, morally unregulated world in which they live, with clarity and integrity, illuminated by a realization of the ideals to which the gospel calls them.

Pastoral care in practice: community bereavement

One school chaplain quoted earlier referred to 'finding those who are lost and helping them to feel found, to be found, to heal'; but a chaplain's pastoral care in schools isn't just about working individually with students, staff or parents. There is a hugely significant corporate dimension, in which the chaplain may be offering care, reassurance and some sense of corporate spirituality to the whole community. Any tragic event in a school is deeply felt, perhaps especially by students, whose vision of life may well not include the idea of suffering and mortality. At such times of corporate bereavement there is a key role for the chaplain as a representative and embodiment of Christian love and hope.

One chaplain in a church-maintained school described the challenge of devising a form of liturgy to mark the death in a road accident of a Year 10 student, someone entirely unconnected with any faith community except the school itself. Eventually, through consultation with students, a liturgy emerged incorporating the late student's favourite music rather than hymns, and with the only explicitly religious element being a cross symbol marked out in tea-lights. This school's memorial liturgy served as a kind of corporate pastoral care, designed to help the healing of the whole grieving community. A chaplain in an independent boarding school needed to respond to the death of a sixth-form student in a car accident just after Easter. A further student had been severely injured in the accident and the car had been driven by another student: emotional responses were confused, the community poised between grief and deep anger. A communal liturgy needed to be devised, and once more light was a key symbol, but in this more explicitly faith-shaped context it was the light of the Paschal candle – the light, as the chaplain put it, 'that shines through and past the darkness of death, the light of hope'.

The grief and anger of this student community, enhanced by the fact that the driver of the car had been drinking and that the injured student lay apparently dying in hospital, had somehow to be lived with and managed, says the chaplain, for the whole of that half term at least:

> The level of grief in the community was almost overwhelming at times. Students could barely comprehend how someone so vibrant and life-giving could be snatched away from them, someone who was poised on the edge of an exciting life . . . I recognized that many of the pupils and staff projected on to me their angers and their hopes. I was to blame for this tragedy, yet they needed me more than ever, because I was also the symbol of hope.

Another chaplain, in a church academy, speaks of a similar incident and of how the opportunity for students of going to the chapel and lighting a candle and 'just sitting and wondering "Why?"' was perceived as a healing response to the death of their fellow-student. This chaplain also describes how it emerged, following a student's loss of her mother, that a number of other students had been similarly bereaved. This led to the chaplain holding in the week before Mothering Sunday a lunchtime liturgy to remember mothers and grandmothers, offering the opportunity for both staff and students to light candles, to pray, to reflect and to grieve. In another church academy the chaplain describes the challenges of responding to bereavement like this:

> The biggest challenge is helping teenagers navigate their own sense of loss while they also try to support other members of their family; when say a dearly loved grandparent dies it is not unusual for a student to bury their own grief at home in an attempt to support their parent. School then becomes their safe place to express grief, at least in the short term. For many I support this is their first experience of a close relative dying, so learning to grieve well is of real importance.

These narratives are a reminder that – as Paul Avis insists – the pastoral ministry of the Church is at the forefront of mission. Death, loss and bereavement are events which call out for a sense of meaning and for comfort, notably among the young, whose understanding of life and death may not be as sophisti-cated – or as cynical and blasé – as that of the adult generation. In responding to death in the school community, a chaplain may be both the leader of public liturgy – often devised and shaped with students – and the one offering personal comfort; both the one to blame and the symbol of hope. It is the chaplain who, in the midst of tragedy and all the confused and tumul-tuous feelings it prompts, must somehow publicly signify to the school community the Christian belief that love is stronger than death, that there is a loving purpose in the universe, and that if we dare say anything about God, it is that God is Love.

Pastoral care in practice: accompanying the spiritual journey

St Augustine wrote: 'We make our way like pilgrims on a jour-ney, people of no fixed abode; we are on the road, yet not home; still aiming for our goal, though yet to arrive' (Atwell 2004, p. 417). The image of the journey is deeply embedded in the Judaeo-Christian tradition. The wanderings of the people of Israel in the desert, the itinerant ministry of Jesus, the apostolic missionary journeys: all these resonate onwards from their biblical origins; 'for here we have no lasting city, but we seek the city that is to come' (Heb. 13.14). The image of the spiritual journey or pilgrimage seems a natural one for chaplains in school to use, and as we saw in Chapter 3, it was a dominant metaphor for Sister Mary McKeone in describing her chaplaincy work.

Adolescence certainly has journey-like characteristics. For any secondary school student it is uncharted: a pilgrimage no one else has taken in quite this way, with its direction uncertain and its destination unknown until arrival. It is increasingly hazardous, for those of either sex, and – to adopt an image used by John Bunyan – along the way there are sloughs of despond: some 30 per cent of English adolescents have sub-clinical mental health problems (Bunting 2014). The church school should, it is arguable, be a more supportive context for undertaking this journey than others, and there is a crucial place for chaplaincy as 'presence', in offering to 'walk alongside' students, as Sister Mary describes it, 'listening and reflecting with them in such a way that they will deepen their perception of God in their lives (McKeone 1993, p. 97).

In the ethos of the church school this image of the spiritual journey is a natural one. It is a journey towards adulthood, at one level; a journey towards full human flourishing; a journey towards an adult spirituality – and even possibly towards faith. It involves for any secondary school student the shaping of personal values and identity, the formation of personal habits of life, the exploration of life's significance. The image of accompaniment is also a powerful one. It suggests not that the journey of the spirit is in some way already completed for the chaplain, that here is someone who has found the answer to all life's issues, but rather that the chaplain continues to be 'on the way' and therefore someone who can genuinely accompany others on their journeys. For Sister Mary, therefore, the kind of question a chaplain should constantly be asking is: 'What is happening in me? How am I being changed by my experience?' To accompany others on their journeys implies being open to self-scrutiny, alert to change, eager to continue exploring the spiritual realm. As one chaplain said:

> I've felt as probably we all feel that faith is a journey, and if I'm alongside someone for a little bit of their journey . . . that's OK, I've just been a part of that hundred yards for them.

One biblical narrative conveys luminously what 'accompaniment' may mean. In Luke's Gospel the narrative of the Passion occupies the penultimate chapter and is followed by the Resurrection narratives of the last chapter. The largest part of this final chapter is given to the story of the Emmaus road: two disciples of Jesus, one named Cleopas, the other unnamed, have left Jerusalem following the discovery of the empty tomb 'on the first day of the week' (Luke 24.1). The risen Christ draws near, joining them on the road, unrecognized, and walks with them towards Emmaus; and it is not long before the three fall into conversation. Jesus asks questions of the disciples, encouraging them to explain their understanding of the Jerusalem events, and after listening to their account of 'all these things that had happened', offers a scriptural interpretation of the suffering of the Messiah. Invited to join the two at supper as they stop for the night at an inn, Jesus presides at the table and carries out the eucharistic actions: he takes bread, blesses God, breaks the bread and gives it. He is recognized in these actions but vanishes from the disciples' sight.

Perhaps no better account of chaplaincy exists in the Scriptures. Here is a dominical ministry, in which drawing near to others, walking with them and inviting them into conversation is the prelude to any offering of interpretation or understanding of events on the minister's part. It is a ministry so humanly attractive that it prompts an invitation to eat together at table; and only when this quasi-liturgical moment is reached does the Lord reveal himself in the 'breaking of the bread'. This is person-focused ministry, open and exploratory, rooted in mutual exchange, sealed with a sacred moment of sacramental recognition. And when insight comes, the minister moves on – his journey continues. 'Who is the third who walks always beside you?', asks T. S. Eliot in *The Waste Land* (1963, p. 77). The haunting sense evoked by the poet of an accompanying spiritual presence on the road reminds us of the presence of Christ in our own pilgrimages; but also of the possibility and the significance of the presence of a chaplain accompanying the young on theirs. Pastoral care in schools – the heart of chaplaincy ministry – is ultimately about the accompanied spiritual journey.

7

Celebrating the Sacred:
Accessing the Spiritual Dimension

For the church school students interviewed in the Bloxham/
OxCEPT research project it was self-evident that chaplains have
chapels – the etymological connection is unavoidable, whatever
the precise origins of the term may be (see MacCulloch 2009).
Chief among the tasks of a chaplain, in their view, was what
students variously referred to as 'taking the services', 'leading
assemblies', 'doing the Eucharists' – the different terms indicating something of the range of schools' own varying ecclesial
cultures. And for those practising as chaplains in schools, what
I have called their liturgical function ranked equally highly.
Not simply a pastoral carer, a chaplain in the school context
is inevitably seen as, and conscious of being, someone a major
part of whose role is to lead others in worship.

Worship in church schools: setting the scene

What, though, do we mean when we speak of 'worship' in the
school context? There's a confusion of terms in use. As we saw
in Chapter 3, the law still speaks of the duty of all maintained
schools to have a daily act of 'collective worship'; schools themselves commonly use the term 'assembly' instead of 'collective
worship'; and for some independent church schools the term
'chapel' covers both daily – or less frequent – 'prayers' and
weekly celebrations of the Eucharist. Many maintained church
schools and academies have tutor-group prayers (or times of

reflection) when formal 'assembly' – very often for practical reasons – is not able to be held; and a further dimension is the provision in all kinds of church school of opportunities for voluntary worship. These services – for example pre-school or lunchtime prayers or Eucharist, evening Compline – will usually be attended by small numbers of staff and students.

The picture is further enriched by the seasonal nature of the Church's year and the dynamics of the school calendar. Some church schools hold special Founders' or Commemoration services, to which there will be invitations to governors and local dignitaries. There may be special Christmas or Easter services, or services to mark Lent or Advent or All Saints' Day or the feast of a saint specially linked with the school. Most church schools will also have special services to mark the completion of studies at GCSE or A level – 'leavers' services'. And if the school or the wider world is afflicted by tragedy or loss, there may be special acts of worship to gather the community together in mourning and reflection.

Across the whole range of church schools, then, there is a wide spectrum of worship practice, and also inevitably of worship styles. And while some church schools have worship co-ordinators whose task is distinct from a pastorally focused chaplaincy, it is likely that chaplains have the leading role in shaping school worship across the spectrum of church schools. The nature and style of that worship will depend heavily on the chaplain's own background, tradition and personal spirituality, and on the school's own tradition. In some schools there will be informal styles of worship: student music groups may lead worship songs rather than traditional hymns; there may also be a prominent place for multi-media presentations and projected visual imagery. In others, worship may tend instead to formality and tradition, with choir anthems and hymns, a highly structured liturgy, a focus on the altar and traditional visual symbols.

The overall picture of worship in church schools is highly diverse – but in each school community it will be understood as the ordinary way of doing things, the recognized culture, simply 'what we do here'. This means that the particular way students experience worship in church schools is highly dependent on context – and notably, as suggested above, on the tradition and practice of their particular school and the approach of their chaplain. The very nature of 'worship' as experienced and understood by students will be determined by the chaplain as a designer and leader of that worship.

Equally significant, however, is the nature of the chapel or place of worship itself. These vary widely. Many independent church schools have a large, traditionally ordered chapel, inherent to the school's design and highly suitable for corporate and public worship. Chapels like this are significant public statements of the place of faith in the school but may be less appropriate for smaller numbers of worshippers or for informal liturgies, though a side- or lady-chapel may provide for these. In maintained church schools there is usually less generous provision. It is rare to have a large chapel, able to hold a significant portion of the school community, unless this is incorporated into the assembly hall. More characteristically, the chapel is a separate space designed for a smaller number of worshippers. It may be an insignificant space, relatively anonymous and unatmospheric; or it may be more imaginatively furnished and decorated, a deliberately created, evocative 'sacred space' central to the school's life, attractive to students and staff as a place of calm and profundity.

So the school's chaplain (as well as its architecture and design) powerfully shapes the nature of the place of worship (the sacred space) and its atmosphere. In effect, chaplains act as gatekeepers to the spiritual dimension of the school community's life, particularly as this is expressed in assemblies and worship. How chaplains have themselves experienced worship, and what makes worship real for them, is of huge importance. So too is how well they understand the students for whom worship is designed, how much they are able to gauge what 'works' best for them, what makes the spiritual dimension most accessible. One lay chaplain in a church academy says:

> At its best, our worship aims to transcend the here and now through colour, music, art, participation, keen thinking, and, most counterculturally for the streaming generation, silence.

Theological perspectives on worship

So far I have used the word 'worship' to cover a range of possibilities: a celebration of the Eucharist, formal services for special occasions, less formal services, the daily school assembly, classroom prayers – in fact anything in the school context that involves corporate and public prayer. These two features, the corporate and the public, are identified by the theologian and liturgist Gabriel Hebert as central to Christian worship. In his *Liturgy and Society* (Hebert 1961), Hebert centres his attention on the Eucharist – which from his stance is Christian worship par excellence – as essentially the public and communal declaration of the Christian mystery of salvation, the eucharistic liturgy both expressing, displaying and enacting the Church's theology. It has, however, been characteristic of much Christian thinking for 'theology' and 'liturgy' to be seen as distinct and separate disciplines or thought-silos – as if liturgy (how we worship) has no particular connection with theology (how we believe). Hebert challenges this model, arguing for a unitive vision of theology and liturgy, the latter enacting and giving shape to the former.

Given such an approach, each school needs a clear espoused theology of worship, an explanation of its worship practice. At the root of the varying theologies of worship espoused by school chaplains interviewed in the research project was the common conviction that worship in schools should be designed to create the possibility of genuine encounter with God. This core conviction, however, is expressed in widely differing ways. The spectrum of approach is perhaps best indicated by identifying two contrasting 'ideal types' of theology of worship espoused by school chaplains.

School chaplains of more catholic orientation identify the prime locus for the encounter with God in worship as the Eucharist, the declaration and celebration of the Church's faith. One such chaplain expressed this approach in these terms: 'the liturgy can be a transforming experience'. Echoing Hebert's thinking, these chaplains highlight the importance of the public, corporate celebration of the Eucharist in the heart of the school community, a celebration to be carried out with due reverence and the highest possible quality of music, liturgy and ceremonial. The gospel – the whole mystery of salvation – is declared and enacted in the liturgy; here is the meeting point of heaven and earth, the place of encounter; Christ becomes recognized, as in the Emmaus narrative, in 'the breaking of the bread'.

For school chaplains of more evangelical orientation the emphasis is less on the corporate celebration of the Eucharist, more on the place of individual reflection and prayer and the desire for students to respond personally to the biblical vision. School worship from this perspective will be shaped less by the Church's traditional ritual and more by a consciousness that students need at a personal level to grasp the nature of Christian faith for today. So worship may be designed to prompt reflection, to 'open up spiritual truths to people' and enable them to 'interact with [Christian] ideas', as another chaplain said. It may incorporate contemporary music encouraging identification with faith, and will be consciously wrapped within a culturally accessible medium. For such chaplains, the encounter sought is again with the Christ of the Emmaus Road – the one who prompts reflection, breaks open the word. But in both these contrasting models of school worship the same underlying theological impulse is at work: the desire that students should come to understand something of the nature of Christian faith, and experience the possibility of encounter with Christ through word or sacrament.

Worship in school: developing a theology

School chaplains recognize that a minority of their students will come from practising Christian backgrounds, and they are acutely conscious of the different cultural world their students inhabit and also of the countercultural nature of much of what the Christian faith has to say. At the same time they recognize that, as one chaplain said, chaplaincy in schools is 'the Church's largest and most important work among young people'. This view is one also taken by the Jesuit educationalist Michael Holman, a former school chaplain and head teacher and currently principal of Heythrop College, London University. In a recent address to Roman Catholic school chaplains, Holman suggests that: 'Ministry amongst young people in schools is especially significant. For most of the children with whom we work, these schools are, for them and their families, their primary Christian community.' Schools, therefore, 'provide for the Church its principal platform for working with young people because, unlike many of our parishes, we can meet young people and their families there' (Holman 2010).

This understanding of the church school as their 'primary Christian community' for most students – and for their parents – is hugely significant for chaplaincy. It implies that their school chaplain is the Christian minister most students – and many parents – are most likely to meet, echoing the perception of the chaplain quoted earlier, in Chapter 4 (see page 55). It suggests that students' experience of worship in schools is likely to be the most influential they come across, perhaps even their only experience of Christian worship in their teenage years. The nature and quality of the opportunities offered for worship in school will potentially shape students' spirituality for their adult lives. Given this, the role of the chaplain as a theologically informed liturgist, as an expert in worship, is of vital importance.

So how do chaplains in school develop the expertise they need to be the liturgists their students need them to be? This is, as I have suggested, at root about theology – hard theological thinking about what worship is for in the school context, and how worship may best be planned and designed in the particular school community in which the chaplain serves. It is also, though, a sociological question. School chaplains need to have developed real sociological and cultural insight, a deep awareness of the culture from which their students come. As they plan and prepare worship for students – and often *with* students – they must somehow manage to bridge the gap between the world of the gospel and its inherent values and the contemporary world in which students are engaged and by which their value system is significantly formed.

The contribution of sociology: contrasting approaches

The contrasting approaches to worship in school offered as 'ideal types' above depend in effect on different sociological as well as theological impulses. If a more evangelical approach can be seen as seeking the Christ of the Emmaus Road who breaks open the word, it can also be seen to have a particular understanding of culture and the need for cultural relevance. In this understanding – seen at its most developed in 'youth work' styles of relating to young people, and fostered by the Schoolswork organization (Schoolswork 2014) among others – it is seen as essential to approach the young via cultural forms with which they are familiar and in which they are 'at home'. From this perspective, school assemblies will tend to be fashioned using or referencing YouTube clips, popular chart music and similar ingredients, combined so that students will be encouraged to question and think beyond the values of the present culture and begin to explore the spiritual perspective.

The community theologian Ann Morisy's concept of 'apt liturgy' offers an important rationale for this kind of approach, combining both theological and sociological insights. In Chapter 4, I considered her concept of a 'ministry of awakening', aimed to help people realize that 'within our ordinary experiences there are rumours of angels and traces of ultimacy'. This concept links with her idea of 'apt liturgy', and similarly assumes, on the basis of research into religious experience and spirituality (Hay 1998), that while the majority of people will have sensed God's presence in their lives, they will not have any formal theological shaping of this experience and have no specific, theologically structured belief. Unlike formal worship, says Morisy, apt liturgy is not cultic or limited to the context of the church building. Nonetheless, it is about 'helping people to lift their eyes to a Godly horizon' by using common symbols and everyday language to respond to situations where 'people need something that links heaven and earth' (2004, pp. 156–71). So 'apt liturgy' can be an important concept for school assemblies: it suggests a kind of pre-worship, a lifting of heart and mind in which awareness of the spiritual dimension is encouraged without the use of specifically religious language, and in which the common spirituality of people is enriched and extended in the direction of faith. School worship rooted in this kind of understanding will 'begin where the young are' and seek to lead them towards an explicitly spiritual perspective.

A different understanding, which can be seen as supporting a more catholic approach to liturgy, is developed in the thinking of the French sociologist of religion Danièle Hervieu-Léger (2000). Instead of working inductively from the ambient culture towards the possibility of faith, this understanding emphasizes the objective nature of the religious tradition and by implication the need to be related to it and located within it. Hervieu-Léger sees a religion as 'an ideological, practical and symbolic system through which consciousness, both individual and collective, of belonging to a particular chain of belief is constituted, maintained, developed and controlled'. Her concept of 'the chain of belief' or 'chain of memory' is central to her understanding of religion: a faith community is one that continues through time, largely through the process of recalling its past 'which gives meaning to its present and contains its future'. She notes that the practice of *anamnesis*, of the recalling of the past, is most often observed as a rite; and her model is clearly the Christian rite of the Eucharist.

From this perspective it is evident that to participate in the Eucharist is in some sense to be incorporated into the community of recollection, the collective 'chain of memory' that constitutes the Church. Hervieu-Léger sees this as particularly appropriate to the contemporary cultural situation in which, she says, 'individuals are adrift in a universe without fixed bearings. Their world is no longer one they can construct together. Self-fulfilment is now the chief aim, the subjective unification of fragmented experience' (2000, p. 165). Given this shifting and self-focused cultural context, she argues, one way of constructing self-identity is to accept the 'authority of a tradition' and to become incorporated into its continuing lineage, its ongoing community shaped and constituted by the chain of memory. From this standpoint, school worship centres on the Eucharist and other traditional forms, in which the young are invited to participate and into which participation will incorporate them.

These two contrasting sociological understandings chime clearly with the contrasting 'ideal types' of theological understanding of worship I have identified – the evangelical and the catholic. The evangelical impulse may be described as seeking the point at which contemporary culture can be seen as a 'way in' to the spiritual realm, and by opening up this realm to explore the possibility of individual, spiritual development as students encounter the Christ who breaks open the word. The catholic impulse can be characterized as asserting the objective authority and tradition of the ongoing community of the Church, and inviting participation in its worship and life through engagement with the Eucharist, an encounter with the Christ of the Emmaus Road who is recognized in the breaking of the bread. The more evangelical approach highlights the individual search for faith; the catholic a more communal understanding in which the priority is to become incorporated in the ongoing community through participation in its rituals.

These ideal types may seldom be seen in their extreme form – although during the course of the research project I did encounter both. What seems crucial is that schools think through their own approach to school worship and have a serious rationale that underpins their practice. It may well be that the most effective strategy is to combine insights from both perspectives, adopting a both/and rather than either/or outlook. Such an approach would recognize the cultural distance of most young people from the Church's traditional rituals and would seek to provide 'apt liturgy' as a basic ingredient of school assemblies. It would also at the same time, however, recognize that the Church is an ongoing community of faith rooted in historic events and continuing through time by celebrating and recalling those events. Hence the core liturgy of the Church – the Eucharist – can play a vital part in not only telling the 'story' of Christian faith but also in inviting the commitment of those seeking an identity through community.

Developing religious literacy

If all worship in the school context can be seen fundamentally as an attempt to offer students a place of potential encounter, an entrance-point into the spiritual world, at another level it has a pragmatic function in contributing to the development of religious literacy – a key concept in the current, secular and multi-faith situation of twenty-first-century Britain. By religious literacy I mean the accumulated knowledge and experience that enable students to understand the nature of religious belief and to have some insight into what characterizes the beliefs, practices and lifestyles of various faith communities. In addition, mature religious literacy includes an empathic grasp of what belonging to a faith community might mean for its members; how it might feel to see the world in this way and to live accordingly.

Whether or not a student wishes to participate actively in worship in the school context (and although students were once sanctioned for non-participation, this seems inappropriate in our current age), worship can be seen as an essential part of the curriculum the church school offers. Assemblies where students are invited to think about and to reflect upon issues of justice, fairness, meaning and purpose, and are encouraged to be aware of the lives of others, can contribute significantly to their religious literacy. Similarly, being present at celebrations of the Eucharist without being an active believer can give students an awareness of the nature and meaning of faith and worship in the Christian tradition. While the major factor in developing students' religious literacy may be the quality of a school's RE programme, faith cannot simply be grasped as a reality from the outside. Some 'way in' to the nature of religious experience and the life of faith is also needed, and worship in school can be a context in which such inwardness is developed.

Many of the chaplains I interviewed as part of the Bloxham/ OxCEPT research project emphasized the time they spent in the preparation of school assemblies. Ready-made assembly material is hard to find, limited and not specifically designed for the community served by the chaplain. Preparing PowerPoint presentations is time-consuming, as is preparation for speaking or preaching. One chaplain said:

> I always regard assemblies and what we do in church as really key to what I'm doing . . . I always spend a lot of time preparing assemblies, and it's the same for preaching, because I think that if you are going to talk to anybody and they are going to have to listen . . . you really have to prepare and get a message across to them.

Evidently school chaplains have much to think about in the preparation of collective worship. How will this assembly or service nurture the faith and understanding of students who are practising Christians? How will it contribute to the development of the religious literacy of the non-practising majority? How will it help form people who have a mature grasp of the dynamics of faith? Or, in simpler terms, and to quote a formula of Robert Runcie's highlighted in the Dearing Report: how will it 'nourish those of the faith; encourage those of other faiths; challenge those who have no faith' (Dearing 2001, p. 4)? The demands placed upon a chaplain to design and present worship that is a suitable response to this multiple task are considerable: she or he needs imagination, insight, depth of personal spirituality and a wide repertoire; and above all perhaps, sheer time to find the best content for worship and the best ways to present it. Enabling students to develop a mature level of religious literacy is among a chaplain's most demanding callings.

Religious socialization and school ethos

Closely linked to the concept of religious literacy is that of religious socialization. If religious literacy is about developing a felt understanding of the meaning of faith in practice, religious socialization is the process of being shaped by the expectations and behaviours of religious faith, a process of induction into the world of a particular faith community and, in the case of the church school, the faith community of the Church. Although the Dearing Report does not use the term, 'religious socialization' is in fact the notion underlying much of what it says about the function of church schools. 'Christian values and principles will run through every area of school life', says Dearing; pupils will 'not only learn about religion but . . . experience it as a living tradition and inheritance of faith' (2001, pp. 12, 13). The church school, in other words, is intended to be a place where the young are religiously socialized.

The Dearing Report, as we saw earlier, is clear that a key agent of this process is the church school's distinctive ethos, the deep-structured culture that shapes social habits and relationships in the community. Ethos is experienced and evidenced dynamically in the school's social relationships; that is, in how members of the community relate to and treat one another, what their working assumptions and social habits are. But ethos is also formally stated, expounded and presented in the context of school worship, where the values of the school's

culture are most evidently and publicly displayed and celebrated. As one chaplain said:

> Leading the school in the worship of God, I . . . have an
> opportunity to articulate from my point of view . . . the
> primary values I would want to commend to pupils, so I am
> one of the ways in which [the school] articulates Christian
> values and tries to contribute to the spiritual formation, the
> moral formation, of pupils.

Hence the importance for school chaplains of the preparation
of materials and liturgies for assemblies and classroom worship. It is in the regular, daily worship of the school, in its
liturgy, that its values are shared as students corporately
encounter readings from the Scriptures, prayers deriving from
them, reflections based upon them. It is in the liturgy of the
school that students hear the teaching of Jesus. Whether this is
in the context of the reading of the Gospel passage in a formal
Eucharist or simply as a brief saying projected on the screen
to prompt reflection during an assembly thought of as 'apt
liturgy', it is in the school's worship that students are exposed
to the gospel.

It is also in the context of worship that students learn about
prayer and reflection. To join in the corporate praying of the
Lord's Prayer is to share in the fundamentals of Christian spirituality, to be shaped by it and to acquire a sense of what prayer
is in the Christian understanding: praying the Lord's Prayer is
formative. To experience as listeners or participants some of
the other great formal prayers of the Christian tradition is to
have one's understanding of faith deepened. To share in times
of corporate, silent prayer or reflection, prompted perhaps by
visual images or by words from the Scriptures or from other
spiritual sources, is to learn about the process of prayer and
contemplation. School worship is the place where both the values and the spiritual practices on which the school's life is built
are taught – not as an imposition of belief but as a spiritual
path onto which students are invited.

School worship and spiritual capital

Another way of understanding this is to say that the experience of school worship is designed to increase the spiritual capital students have at their disposal. The concept of spiritual capital, introduced in Chapter 2, derives ultimately from the thinking of Pierre Bourdieu, who understands 'capital' to be not just economic wealth as Marx assumed but also the non-material resources, the social and cultural capital with which people develop and retain their position in society (McLaughlin 2005). In exploring the idea of spiritual capital, the William Temple Foundation researched how churches contribute to their localities and the wider society, concluding that 'spiritual capital' constitutes the motivating basis of faith, belief and values that shapes the actions of faith communities, a resource that individuals and faith groups can access for their own personal well-being but also 'donate' as a gift to the wider community (Baker and Skinner 2006).

But if we see spiritual capital as an inner resource that may both sustain the individual and benefit society through social action, the question remains: how is it acquired? The William Temple Foundation study identifies the faith community itself as the repository of spiritual capital, the bank that allows church members to draw on its resource to support, guide and energize their living. This illuminating approach helps us understand the wider, social significance of school worship. We may see the experience of living in the church school community, and particularly of participating in its corporate worship – where its deepest values and commitments are shared and celebrated – as contributing specifically to the spiritual capital of school members. So – to paraphrase the Dearing Report – a core intention of the church school is simply to endow its students with spiritual capital. This means – rather than setting out to convert them to personal faith – providing through developing students' religious literacy a sufficient understanding of faith and faith-based attitudes, and through corporate worship a sufficient personal experience of faith practices such as prayer and reflection, to provide the inner spiritual resource with which to face both personal and social challenges.

So school worship can be at once both a reaching out towards the Transcendent (Jones et al. 1980, p. 6), the place of possible encounter with the Christ of the Emmaus Road, and the locus for the acquisition of spiritual capital. School worship potentially offers a threefold direction of movement: 'upwards' towards God; inwards, towards the inner self of all participants; and outwards, towards society. The role of the school chaplain in planning, designing and leading corporate worship can be seen as a potentially life-changing one; for 'the liturgy can be transformative'. And whether the chaplain's own understanding of worship leans towards the evangelical or catholic ideal type described above, whether the school's preferred style is formal or informal, the underlying purpose is to enable students to become more aware of God, of their own selves and of others – and of the needs of the wider world.

This is why, for many school chaplains, offering students the opportunity of serving the wider community is a priority. Whether this is in the form of local social service – visiting the housebound, serving tea at the hospice, tidying the gardens of the disabled; or in the more exotic context of service to an impoverished community in Africa through voluntary teaching or school renovation – it is clear that for school students to encounter poverty and disadvantage can be a transformative spiritual experience. As one study in *Religion and Youth* (Collins-Mayo and Dandelion 2010) describes, the experience of young pilgrims to Lourdes demonstrates that working with the disabled and terminally ill can be 'a place to grow spiritually and socially'. School worship has the potential to prompt outward-directed care as well as inner, spiritual development. And equally, the experience of service to others has the potential to prompt spiritual awareness – meeting Christ may take place not only on the Emmaus Road but also in the place of need and suffering, on the way of the cross.

The church school as church

In some ways, therefore, the school may be seen as a kind of church, committed to both worship and service, as Michael Holman's thinking implies (Holman 2010). This perception is one that Rowan Williams explored in an address to Anglican school heads in 2003, in which he reflected on 'the idea of a church school as itself a kind of church'. Williams, along with Holman, takes as his starting-point the fact 'that very many students in a church school will have their primary exposure to shared religious activity in school'. This means, he argues, that 'What the school does corporately as a Christian body will be, to all intents and purposes, how these parents and students will experience the reality of Church.' And 'Church', he goes on to suggest, 'signifies what happens when the presence of Jesus Christ holds people together in a mutual relationship'.

The former archbishop goes on to argue that: 'A church secondary school that is not manifestly rooted in eucharistic community is less than it might be . . . . [T]he church school's culture . . . can provide a crucial experience of what the Body of Christ means, for those, adults and young people, who would not otherwise see it' (Williams 2004, pp. 7–9). If we add the testimony of the Anglican archbishop and the Jesuit academic together, we accumulate a powerful argument for a vision of the church school as church, and for church as characterized essentially by its being an inclusive, worshipping, eucharistic community. From the perspective of spirituality, and from the perspective of holistic Christian education, worship is the most significant activity of the church school. It is as a school community comes inclusively together to worship – and to worship in the fundamental Christian way eucharistically – that it becomes fully a community. The task of designing and shaping worship devolves upon the school chaplain, who has the immense privilege and responsibility of so conducting worship that for all in the community their experience is genuinely one of being in the house of God, and at the gate of heaven.

8

School Chaplaincy:
A Complex Professional Role

The core tasks of school chaplaincy, as we have seen, are pastoral and liturgical, and animating both these functional aspects of the role is the essential, ontological nature of chaplaincy as a ministry of being, of presence. A chaplain in school represents Christ, ministers to others in the name of Christ, and through worship seeks to provide the opportunity of encounter with Christ. Committed to the well-being, human flourishing and spiritual development of school students and the wider school community of parents and staff, she or he is called to a self-giving ministry that is both multi-dimensional and fundamental to the nature of church school education. A church school without chaplaincy seems almost a contradiction in terms; and there is something profoundly amiss in any church-school context where chaplaincy comes low on the list of financial priorities. If the spiritual mission of the church school counts for anything, and if the Church of England is truly interested in anything more than simply having a stake in the education system, then chaplaincy in schools must be a major priority. Church schools need chaplains.

But the multi-dimensional nature of this ministry – a complex, professional role – now needs further exploration, and having considered its pastoral and liturgical core I shall now turn to further aspects of what chaplaincy in schools involves. The Bloxham Project/OxCEPT research programme, as we saw earlier, identified four further functional dimensions of school chaplaincy – the **spiritual, missional, prophetic** and **pedagogic** dimensions – and I shall now consider each of these in more detail.

The spiritual dimension of school chaplaincy

In our national online survey the spiritual function of school
chaplaincy was ranked highly: it clearly has a strong presence
in the practice and consciousness of working school chaplains.
One chaplain interviewed, when describing this dimension of
his work in a church comprehensive school, suggested that
his first duty was to be a 'prayerful presence' within the community, someone whose personal spirituality was evidenced
in all his interactions with students or staff colleagues. Other
chaplains echoed this emphasis, referring to the importance of
prayer in their personal and professional lives. Many of those
interviewed said that beginning the day in school with prayers
said in the chapel, sometimes with other members of the school
staff, was what provided the spiritual grounding for their day's
work. One chaplain referred tellingly to prayer being 'in the
background of all that's going on', describing how in every different conversation and in teaching there was for him 'a sense
of prayer', even when events meant he had no chance of stop-
ping, closing his eyes and putting his thoughts into words.

It might be expected that school chaplains rate prayer, often
shared with others, and a sense of prayerfulness brought to
conversations and relationships, as significant in sustaining both their inner, personal life and their ministerial focus.
These are, after all, spiritual professionals. But it is not just at
a personal level that school chaplains seek to be spiritual. For
many, there is a clear consciousness of exercising a spiritual
leadership function in the school community. In one sense this
is self-evident, as chaplains will usually preside over worship,
lead assemblies and conduct services marking special events in
a school's life. But less evidently, chaplains are conscious of
being seen – as a parish priest may still be in a more traditional
rural, village community – as the person who represents the
spiritual realm, who will be expected to have an answer to people's deep questionings over suffering or disaster or who will
at least find the right words to say when any kind of public
pronouncement seems required by events that in some sense

shake the community's spiritual foundations. One chaplain I interviewed said that students in his school simply called him 'vicar'.

There are also likely to be times when the school chaplain feels impelled to stand for spiritual values and aspirations, when she or he senses these may be under threat. One chaplain interviewed referred to situations of tension, times when the school's preoccupations seemed very different from his own. Identifying a popular cult of 'success' as a common ideal among students and staff, but insisting that life and school are just not 'all about success', he went on: 'The Christian gospel is saying one thing, and the vocabulary of the school might be saying another.' One aspect of spiritual leadership in a school community is discerning such tensions between the values of the public square and those of the gospel, and having the clarity of mind and sheer tact to be able expose them to colleagues, perhaps especially to school leaders – a matter of simply opening up new realization and prompting a heightened spiritual awareness. Similarly, one chaplain talks of the moments 'when I realize that a young person has started to see beyond themselves to God/others/the spiritual dimension'. Here is a ministry of spiritual awakening.

The missional dimension of school chaplaincy

Research showed too that school chaplains are deeply conscious of being part of the *missio Dei*, the divine mission to the world, and of seeking to reveal the divine purpose of love within all things. In a context where, as one chaplain put it, 'the primary language is not religious language' and the dominant mode of response to the world around us is secular, part of the chaplain's missional function is this ministry of awakening, helping people to see beyond the everyday, beginning the work of disclosing traces of the divine presence. This is for school chaplains about finding the grace to encourage students – and staff – to lift their eyes and sense the sacred; for as Ann Morisy insists, 'In a materialistic, earthbound culture we have to do prior work before people can contemplate the presence of God' (2004, pp. 146, 159).

This 'prior work' of mission involves a process of re-enchantment – helping others to see the world as replete, not with fairies and witches but with real spiritual significance. The Jesuit poet G. M. Hopkins exemplifies this realization: for him, 'The world is charged with the grandeur of God' (1947, p. 70); and chaplains are in the business of prompting a recognition that the world of nature and the human world are more than just a set of material phenomena, that the material world truly is 'charged', animated with the life of God. The school chaplain is someone whose presence, influence and specific work are about prompting in students and staff a realization of spiritual reality. Part of this is promoting the awareness that religious language, through its metaphor and symbol, may be descriptive of reality, that it can be truth-telling, truth-revealing.

The given heritage of the Christian tradition – in the Scriptures, hymns, prayers and rituals of the faith – is not immediately accessible to many in the current context, part of the significant loss of connection with the tradition that developed in the later part of the twentieth century. One of the challenges of school chaplaincy is to help people reconnect with the tradition, and the prior work related to this is about prompting a process of reconnection, one which, as Hervieu-Léger would say, needs to be made with the 'chain of memory' (2000). So in one inner-city church school, where there is no set of religious admissions criteria in operation and incoming students are effectively largely unchurched, bringing wisdom from the tradition – in the form of sayings, stories, prayers, songs and ritual actions – into the present life of the community through assemblies is a priority. Finding and forging links between the situations and crises of today as students and staff experience them, and the religious tradition expressed in narrative and liturgy, is a significant part of this reconnection.

This missional dimension of school chaplaincy inevitably takes place in a multi-faith context, wherever the church school is situated, and whatever its own degree of ethnic and religious diversity. Our national survey revealed that more than half of the school chaplains responding (52 per cent) felt they were seen as faith leaders by students of minority faith groups, and that these students sought their help and advice in that role. In one church boarding school the chaplain meets regularly with Muslim students on Fridays for discussion and reflection, in the absence of an imam; in another, a Muslim student affirmed the role of the chaplain in responding to the spiritual needs of other-faith students such as himself. Just as much as the prior work of re-enchantment and reconnection, this is missional chaplaincy: in Archbishop Runcie's terms, 'encouraging those of other faiths' (Dearing 2001, p. 11).

What of the school chaplain's role in relation to student Christian groups? The Runcie formula suggests that young Christians need to be nurtured in the school context, but the national survey showed that three-quarters (75 per cent) of responding chaplains felt a degree of unease about working with school Christian Unions (CUs). One reason for this may be that CUs both at school and university levels still tend to be overseen by para-church organizations of a distinctively conservative outlook, particularly in relation to understandings of the nature and authority of the Bible (see Scripture Union 2014; UCCF 2014). A history of difficult relationships between CUs and other organizations both Christian and secular may be a further factor (see Ekklesia 2007); but in the current post-Christian societal context, any apparent infighting between different groups of practising Christians is counterproductive to mission. It is bewildering at least for school students to observe chaplains and school Christian groups eyeing one another with caution.

Part of the chaplain's missional role, therefore, is to build bridges between his or her own spirituality and theology and the quite probably less sophisticated understanding of young practising Christians in the school. One lay chaplain describes his difficulty in getting alongside students whose church communities remain committed to the literal truth of the six-day creation story; and one task of the chaplain could be seen as helping students of all denominational backgrounds to understand that there is a wide spectrum of Christian outlook and belief, and to help expand their limited horizons in this respect. Similarly, chaplains can be seen as religious or spiritual professionals who foster spiritual growth and development, recognizing the dynamic nature of faith and nurturing an understanding of how questioning may be an aspect of growing faith maturity. Part of the specifically apologetic function of the chaplain may be to mediate between different perceptions of the nature of Christian faith, as well as between the world of secularity and the world of belief.

The prophetic dimension of school chaplaincy

The prophetic dimension of school chaplaincy was first identified in *A Dictionary of Pastoral Care* (Campbell 1987), an article in which looked at chaplaincy in independent schools. Emphasizing the role of chaplains in these schools as 'a living reminder of the [school's] Christian foundation and ethos', the article went on to describe a school chaplain as 'a prophet and a conscience' (Marsh 1987). Our research showed chaplains from across the whole spectrum of church schools affirming this stance. The chaplain quoted above who highlighted differences between the Christian gospel and 'the language of the school' was clearly speaking from a spiritual perspective but also from a prophetic one, as were the chaplains quoted earlier in Chapter 4 who expressed their concerns about possible tensions between a school's Christian values and its educational outlook and practice.

Such tensions may be multiple. Even if we were to remove from consideration the technical and professional aspects of education – the content of the curriculum, appropriate teaching strategies for different age groups and ability levels and so on – much of the rest of a school's life remains open for questioning; and at its root, a prophetic stance is prompted by questioning the way things are. In any church school there may be aspects of educational practice or community life that deserve to be questioned. How are students encouraged or incentivized to learn well? How are they managed and disciplined? How much priority is given to pastoral care? How much is the school concerned with developing the character and disposition of students? How are staff managed and with what degree of empathy and human understanding? What are the deep impulses, the aspirations and ambitions that animate the school's life, and how far are they in accord with the Christian values and foundation of the school?

What at its core is the school teaching about life and how it should be lived? The grammar school I attended in the 1960s was described by one of its former students, a writer and educational commentator, as teaching two central things: snobbery and conservatism. Perhaps every school has its own implicit, core messages, and if the chaplain can truly be described as a 'prophet and a conscience', part of his or her role is to keep the school under observation from the perspective of Christian values, to identify the school's implicit agenda and expose it to scrutiny. But this is a delicate matter: one non-teaching chaplain, enthusiastically described by her students as an advocate for them and their viewpoint, was concerned lest this perception, being made public, might lessen her standing in the eyes of the school leadership team. Another chaplain, championing the need of a highly disruptive student to remain in school rather than be excluded, had a very hard case to argue with the head, who was only too aware of the ongoing disruption to the school community this student caused.

'Speaking truth to power', which is how we described the prophetic dimension of school chaplaincy in the national survey, is a potentially tricky undertaking: a chaplain who is always knocking on the head's door to champion a cause is unlikely to be popular or even, eventually, listened to. Some chaplains have good, regular access to the head and leadership team, though as we saw earlier only a very small proportion of chaplains enjoy membership of the leadership team and the

high status that goes with this. This raises a number of questions. Is a chaplain in fact best placed when cut off and insu-
lated from the political, personnel and power issues dealt with
at school leadership level? Or is there a case in principle for
a chaplain's presence on the leadership team, perhaps overtly
to act as the voice of conscience? There remains a dilemma
for all appointed chaplains – though the newer brand of para-
chaplains described earlier escape this (see pages 59–60) – about
whether they should be insiders or outsiders to the school's
corridors of power. What is clear is that chaplains in all contexts sense a calling to be a school's conscience, its questioning
and truth-telling prophetic voice.

The chaplain as teacher: the pedagogic dimension

Although school chaplains responding to the national survey
ranked the teaching dimension of their role lowest of the six
identified, it remains an inescapable part of chaplaincy – not
least because through word and action a chaplain is demonstrating what Christian faith is and involves. To care for others
and share their spiritual journeys, to lead worship and open up
a God-space for students and staff: these core chaplaincy functions are a lived demonstration of the life of faith. A chaplain
in school is teaching by example, and the lesson to be learned
will be acutely observed by all in the community.

Beyond this demonstrative or performative aspect of the
chaplain's life, however, there are several respects in which
the chaplain's function is pedagogic. Etymologically a 'guide
for the young', the pedagogue or teacher is charged with the
responsibility of showing the way, illuminating how to live and
what is worth learning. School assemblies provide one instance
of the chaplain as a public teacher. One chaplain recounts a
student's response to an assembly address reported to him
by a fellow student – 'I really need to rethink my life' – and
comments that even if his address hadn't in fact prompted 'an
especial spiritual jump' for the student, it had nonetheless been

evidently received as 'relevant and helpful'. One student at an independent church boarding school, commenting on the benefit of having visiting preachers at the school's weekly corporate Eucharist, said simply: 'They give us life lessons.' And where students may be a critical or sceptical audience – as they perhaps should be towards visiting adults coming with a deliberate message – there will still be engagement with the ideas and perceptions of others. To add a coda to the previous chapter, a chaplain's special responsibility as a teacher in the context of school assemblies is to prompt thoughtful, spiritual response, to initiate questioning, to bring new understanding, fresh realization.

As we saw earlier, one traditional model for chaplaincy in church schools is where the chaplain is also a classroom teacher in addition to the public teaching role involved in leading assemblies and worship. The classroom – even in our age of ubiquitous and advancing educational technology – remains a context above all for personal interaction, at root an encounter between the minds of teacher and students as both engage with the subject of study. As a classroom teacher, a chaplain has the opportunity not only to respond to questioning about faith or religion but also to initiate such reflective questioning, inviting students to explore further, to think outside the terms of their previous understanding through engagement and open discussion.

For a chaplain who teaches RE there is the particular responsibility of developing students' religious literacy in a clear and objective way, enabling real understanding of the features, values and impulses of the world's faiths as well as of the faith embraced by the school. Chaplains who teach in other subject areas have the opportunity to prompt critical reflection about many aspects of human thought and living: about what motivates societies and peoples, what shapes scientific development, what a just social and economic order might be like. In all these contexts, and in those situations where – as happens in some church schools – the chaplain is called in as a consultant to lessons on citizenship, PSHE or sex and relationship education, the chaplain is a teacher: the pedagogic dimension of chaplaincy clearly matters.

The school chaplain may also be in a formal sense a teacher and expositor of the Christian faith, a catechist, especially in those schools that see it as their role to be 'church' for students. Catechesis – the teaching of the faith to those preparing for Christian initiation in baptism or confirmation – is far more than a simple transmission of doctrine, the disciplined learning of a catechism. It is also an exploration of how Christian values relate to contemporary society and culture and of what Christian living involves in practice. An increasing number of church-maintained schools and academies – seeing themselves as their students' 'primary Christian community' (Holman 2010) – now offer catechesis and the rite of confirmation. Long a standard part of independent church school life (though sometimes regrettably seen just as a 'rite of passage'), confirmation now potentially offers the opportunity for students in all kinds of church schools to learn about and commit to the Christian faith, should they choose to do so.

Job descriptions and accountability for school chaplaincy

Given the multi-dimensional nature of school chaplaincy just sketched, how best can the job be defined and described? Our research revealed a wide range of practice in church schools. More than a quarter (28 per cent) of chaplains responding to the online survey said they had no formal, written job description – a worrying figure in a highly professionalized educational culture. There were clear differences between different kinds of school. All those responding from church academies had job descriptions, in some cases setting out their role in considerable detail. Approaching three-quarters of chaplains working in independent church schools (73 per cent) had job descriptions, but in church-maintained schools the percentage was significantly lower (63 per cent), and particularly worrying. The highly professionalized culture of the academies movement is demonstrated in the fact that all academy chaplains had job descriptions. In contrast the relatively low proportion of chaplains with job descriptions in church maintained schools – not much more than half – could indicate a less focused culture in these schools, even one where there is no real clarity about what a chaplain is for or should do.

Job descriptions link closely with accountability, one of the dominant themes in English education since the 1980s. Our survey asked chaplains whether their work was formally reviewed – or appraised – as part of a system of accountability, both within the school and within the external, ecclesial structures of the Church. Responses again gave cause for concern. A quarter of chaplains reported no regular in-school review or appraisal; and while over four-fifths of those in independent schools were reviewed, only just over half (59 per cent) of those in church-maintained schools were. When it came to specifically ecclesial oversight the picture was significantly worse. Fewer than half responding chaplains overall (43 per cent) said their work was reviewed through the Church's diocesan structures: from maintained schools and academies just over half of respondents (56 per cent); but in the independent schools only just over a third (36 per cent). This presents a worrying picture of a significant cadre of school chaplains whose work is both unsupervised and unsupported by their sponsoring body.

There may be a lingering, clerical culture of isolated independence at work here, deriving from the parochial system; but whether such an attitude is appropriate in the twenty-first century is another matter. Contemporary practice in the social and psychiatric professions now assumes both accountability through appraisal, and personal, professional support through 'supervision': it is now axiomatic that an individual social worker or counsellor should not work in isolation but rather have the benefit of professional support. Supervision in this sense provides the context in which professionals can check their own perceptions of their clients' personal and pastoral issues against a colleague's, and where the burdens of personally and psychologically demanding work with individuals and families can be unloaded and shared. A school chaplain's pastoral work will be similarly demanding; and it is a matter of real concern that the Church is not currently providing for chaplains in church schools the degree of professional oversight and support that pastoral supervision can effectively offer (Leach and Paterson 2010).

What seems to be revealed by all this is a significant disconnect between the strategically important work undertaken by chaplains in school and the institutional Church on whose behalf this work is done. It is as if the Church has not yet fashioned an understanding of school chaplaincy clear enough to be able to help shape this ministry as a professional role, to take seriously its oversight and accountability or to provide the personal support it needs. Some chaplains interviewed made very clear their own sense of distance from the institutional Church. One chaplain in a maintained school revealingly noted that she felt her accountability both to God, to 'the bishop at some removed level' but 'obviously predominantly in the school . . . to the head'. Another chaplain, listing those he felt accountable to as 'God, family, pupils, deputy head, head', added: 'I don't really feel very accountable to a bishop, to be honest'; similarly, another chaplain said: 'Who I don't feel particularly accountable to is the Church of England, or . . . my area bishop.'

School chaplains and the wider Church

The distance between school chaplains and the institution of the Church is palpable and keenly felt. The national survey showed that nearly two-thirds (64 per cent) overall of chaplains in Church of England schools felt 'somewhat detached' from the work of their deanery and diocese, a proportion that increased to almost three-quarters (73 per cent) in independent church schools. Nor do school chaplains sense a positive standing for their ministry within the wider ministry of the Church. Only just over a tenth of respondents to the survey (11 per cent) agreed that school chaplaincy was recognized as a 'pioneering ministry' within the

Church; and as one chaplain said: 'I might as well be working as a missionary in a foreign country.' This sense of frustration is described by another chaplain who said: 'the wider Church does not appreciate the missional potential of its schools or of the vital vocational work that is going on in school among young people', a view reinforced by another who said: 'The wider Church does not appreciate the enormous potential for contact with young people that school chaplaincy represents.'

For many school chaplains, then, there is a keen sense of being on the edge of the institutional Church. The positioning of their ministry was variously described by responding chaplains as 'marginal', 'frontier', 'isolated', 'out on a limb', 'separate', the connotations of these varying descriptions ranging from the positive and affirming ('frontier') to the distinctly negative ('out on a limb'). One chaplain interestingly said:

> I am a marginal figure on the edge of the Church but this is a good place to be! It is the only place where the Church meets outsiders. Because I am peripheral to the Church I am the very frontier of its ministry.

This perhaps encapsulates the dilemma for many school chaplains: the Church for and within which their work is undertaken has no clearly affirmative understanding of their ministry, and this places them in a marginal, almost 'outsider' position – one that may be rejoiced in but also may lead to feelings of isolation and neglect. Somehow, the distance between the Church and the school chaplains who minister in its name and on its behalf needs to be narrowed.

The new para-chaplaincy and the traditional model

Newer versions of school chaplaincy – 'para-chaplaincy' – may avoid some of the institutional issues traditional Church of England chaplaincy experiences. Visiting para-chaplains generally work in the context of a local charity where there is a clear sense of specific mission and a small number of active workers, supported by links to local churches. Such enterprises emerge usually from an interdenominational, evangelical context, fostering their sense of mission and purpose, and their young 'schools workers' or para-chaplains appear to be driven by a genuinely pastoral concern that has within it a strongly evangelistic impulse: their aim may be seen as to bridge the worlds of school and church, to bring the young into the sphere of Christ. In one such context I joined a small group of para-chaplains as they regrouped and debriefed at the end of the afternoon: they had come from different schools and had undertaken varying tasks – presenting RE lessons, supporting a lunchtime Christian group, befriending vulnerable students. The depth of their pastoral and evangelistic concern was palpable.

'Dropping in' to schools provides para-chaplains with a degree of freedom of operation and sharpening of focus unavailable to the 'embedded' chaplain. Sharing a similar pastoral concern to that of the Church's own school chaplains, the new para-chaplains have no need to take the role of spiritual leader within the community. They have no obligation to be at the heart of planning and delivering liturgy and worship (though they may lead the occasional school assembly) and they appear to have an understanding of mission that foregrounds evangelization. They are not called to the difficult task of being a prophetic voice within the community of the school, and their pedagogical role is limited. They are not charged with the ongoing responsibility, as one 'embedded' school chaplain described it, of 'being Christ in this place'. Their understanding of chaplaincy, that is, embodies a significantly narrower focus than that of school chaplains in the mainstream Church of England tradition.

Both 'embedded' school chaplaincy as traditionally understood and practised and the new para-chaplaincy offered to non-church schools embody profound Christian motivation, rooted in concern for the other person. They emerge, though, from very different theological spaces. Para-chaplaincy appears to stem from a conservatively inclined theological space where, as H. Richard Niebuhr expresses it, human culture is viewed with suspicion and the task of mission is to bring people out of the world of culture into the world of the Church (see Niebuhr 1951). In contrast, church school chaplaincy moves within a context at least partly shaped by the values and impulses of Christian life and teaching, embodied in the school's ethos: the embedded school chaplain is working to at least some extent within a Christianly-shaped context, one that has a more affirming stance towards human culture as potentially life-enhancing, Christ-conveying and Spirit-inspired.

Conclusion

Chaplaincy in church schools is a complex, multi-dimensional ministry involving the constant exposure of the chaplain to his or her community as the official representative of Christ, the 'God person', a kind of 'walking sacrament', as Austin Farrer memorably writes (Loades and MacSwain 2006). His or her multi-functional role demands a range of qualities: openness, tact, reflectiveness, adaptability, imagination, integrity, theological insight, spiritual depth – among many others. So it does seem astonishing that the framework for this hugely significant and demanding ministry apparently lags so far behind the contemporary professional culture of education within which it is situated, and that chaplains have so little sense of support from the institutional Church on whose behalf this ministry is offered.

The contemporary culture of education assumes a clarity of focus and intention, expressed in clear job descriptions, plain lines of accountability and a structure of oversight, appraisal and support. Our research indicates that these simply do not exist for chaplains across the whole spectrum of church schools. But school chaplains deserve the degree of clarity about their role, the expectation of regular, supportive evaluation of their work and the availability of supportive supervision already axiomatic in the educational and social professions. Much of

this could be provided at school level by heads and governing bodies who valued the chaplain's ministry and saw it as
a key feature of the school's distinctive, Christian ethos. But
there is a challenge here for the national Church to embrace
the significance of school chaplaincy, to recognize its strategic
importance and to provide for those serving in this ministry the
degree of institutional and personal support it currently lacks.

9

Time for Change:
Action on School Chaplaincy

The argument so far . . .

In the opening three chapters of this book I set out to provide the wider context for the ministry of chaplaincy in church
schools. Those chapters looked in turn at Christian mission
and ministry; the nature of contemporary culture; and the spiritual dimension of English education. The argument in these
chapters developed along these lines:

- This is an age in which chaplaincy, as a significant mode
  of authentic Christian ministry, has particular relevance.
  Chaplaincy is 'ministry where people are', a key aspect of
  the Church's mission expressed through word, sacrament
  and pastoral care; its aim is to facilitate human flourishing.
- Our age is a post-Christian era, one in which secular
  assumptions are dominant and there is profound neglect
  of the spiritual dimension of life. While among older people some lingering 'cultural Christianity' survives, among
  the young there is a huge spiritual deficit, a lack of spiritual capital.
- The 'spiritual dimension' was formerly a priority of the
  national education system but in effect is now the serious
  concern only of church schools. The Church of England
  realizes the special and distinct place of its schools as central to its mission but has so far failed to understand the key
  significance of the ministry of chaplains in these schools.

In Chapters 4 to 8 I drew on the Bloxham/OxCEPT school chaplaincy research project to describe, largely from the perspective of practitioners, what the ministry of school chaplains involves, how it is experienced and what makes it distinctive. The description of this ministry focused particularly on the idea of chaplaincy in schools as a 'ministry of presence'; on student perceptions of the nature and value of school chaplaincy; on spiritual pastoral care as the key priority for school chaplains; on the school chaplain's role as a liturgist and leader of worship; on the range of further functional dimensions together making up this complex and multi-faceted ministerial role. In these five chapters, in addition to drawing on research data I drew also on a range of correlating theological sources to present an understanding of school chaplaincy compiled from chaplains' own espoused theology, from formal theological thinking and from the process of theological reflection.

In this final chapter I shall draw together some of the threads of the earlier argument, and in particular consider what the Church of England needs to do about school chaplaincy as a specific mode of ministry and how it can better support, resource, develop and extend chaplaincy in schools as a vital but currently neglected ministry of the Church.

What value for school chaplaincy?

To call school chaplaincy a 'neglected' ministry may sound like special pleading. The fact remains, though, that the latest research reveals that the Church of England has no clear conceptual understanding of chaplaincy as a distinctive ministry, nor even any reliable, factual count of how many chaplains are engaged in active ministry on the Church's behalf (Todd et al. 2014). This picture certainly includes chaplaincy in the Church's maintained secondary schools. The most recent, brief study carried out by the Board of Education and relying on responses from just a third of the Church's maintained secondary schools confirms that the Church has 'no single, accurate, up-to-date central record of those who are school chaplains' (Camp 2014, p. 7). This basic factual uncertainty about the extent of chaplaincy in Church of England schools speaks volumes: if this ministry – and chaplaincy generally – really mattered to the institutional Church, I suspect we should at least have a clearer factual basis on which to build our understanding.

It therefore seems essential for the Church to add to its understanding of chaplaincy, identified earlier as a ministry particularly suited to the cultural conditions of the twenty-first century, and in particular of chaplaincy in schools. There needs to be a recognition at the heart of the Church – which means in effect among its episcopal leaders, in the Archbishops' Council and the General Synod – that the Church's most significant work among and for the young is no longer carried out in Sunday schools and through church youth work in the context of the parish, as was the case in the nineteenth and twentieth centuries, but by chaplains and supporting Christian staff in the context of the church school.

The Bloxham/OxCEPT research project on which I have drawn throughout this book was focused on individual chaplains, lay and ordained, working in church secondary schools. It may be better, however, to think of 'chaplaincy' rather than just of individual chaplains. For while the research made clear the strong sense of individual calling of school chaplains to be the 'God-person', the 'public face of God' and even 'a little Christ' or a 'mini-Jesus' in the context of the school, it is important to recognize that around many or even most chaplains in church schools there will be a penumbra of support. The school staff who meet with the chaplain to share morning prayers, or who attend a weekly lunchtime Eucharist, both support and extend the chaplain's ministry by being seen as confessing Christians in the school. In some schools there may be a formally recognized chaplaincy team. In my own experience of chaplaincy – I was licensed by my bishop as both school head and chaplain – our chaplaincy team included the school's worship co-ordinator, head of music, head of RE and a number of other colleagues with particular pastoral or ministerial skills.

School chaplaincy's extent and potential

Chaplaincy, therefore, may be thought of as a shared and col-
laborative enterprise without undermining the significance of
the individual sense of calling of a designated chaplain. But just
as we have no current factual understanding of the extent of
formal chaplaincy in Church of England schools, we similarly
have no notion of the extent of the supporting penumbra of
other school staff. Nor is there any clear picture of the extent
of informal, visiting chaplaincy offered to schools either by
parish priests or by others engaged in authorized church ministry, such as readers or pastoral assistants. If we look beyond
the Church of England to the range of local charities across
the whole country, such as the Luton Churches Educational
Trust (see page 15), which support para-chaplaincy, the extent
of uncertainty grows. We simply have no idea of the numbers of para-chaplains who are going into non-church schools
for pastoral or evangelistic purposes as representatives of the
Christian faith. All it seems reasonable to suggest is that in
the light of the significance of school chaplaincy as a point of
pastoral and ministerial contact with the young who otherwise
would remain wholly unreached by the churches, the Church
of England should at least properly quantify the extent of chaplaincy ministry in church schools: as I have suggested, the most
recent study only serves to highlight how much we *don't* know
about school chaplaincy, even in the Church of England's own
secondary schools (Camp 2014).

If, as the Dearing Report argued, schools are at the heart of
the Church's mission (2001), it must be time for the Church to
develop and share a clear and positive policy about chaplaincy
in schools. The Church's lack of an intentional policy, a positive theology for school chaplaincy, is in stark and worrying
contrast to the developed thinking in Roman Catholic circles,
and also to the energetic and committed work of the charities
offering para-chaplaincy to schools. School chaplaincy appears
not to matter to the institutional Church. At the very least,
the Church should now strongly encourage all its secondary

schools to plan for the employment of full-time, theologically educated and pastorally trained chaplains.

In short, the institutional Church's perception of chaplaincy in schools needs to change: this vital ministry needs to be seen as positioned at the very centre of the Church's mission to the young. This involves the Church at least establishing the current extent of chaplaincy in its own schools; developing a strong and positive theological understanding of, and policy for, school chaplaincy; encouraging the appointment of full-time chaplains as a matter of urgent priority in all church secondary schools; and developing chaplaincy provision in its primary schools. Church schools in both the primary and secondary phases are the places where unchurched parents may experience 'church' – 'what happens' as Rowan Williams describes it, 'when the presence of Jesus Christ holds people together in a mutual relationship' (Williams 2004).

Beyond church schools

Beyond the Church's own schools, which are its prime responsibility, there is also the question of how the Church may best respond to the pastoral needs of the young in the nation's other schools – the large majority. In these schools, where neither RE nor collective worship can any longer be relied upon to provide even the religious literacy and 'cultural Christianity' that the post-war generation benefited from, the spiritual deficit is even more apparent. Two strategies seem appropriate. First, the Church should strongly encourage local churches through their parish priests and lay ministers to engage actively with schools in their parishes, in an attempt to facilitate chaplaincy for them. While not all schools will welcome this offer of service, if an evidently pastoral rather than evangelistic stance is taken, local churches could find themselves becoming a valuable resource for schools in their area. Second, the Church should engage and collaborate with local para-chaplaincy initiatives where this is not already happening. The institutional

Church in which chaplaincy was first developed as a form of ministry 'where people are' should not keep its understanding of chaplaincy to itself, but instead offer its experience and expertise to para-chaplaincy providers.

Changes in direction: revaluing chaplaincy ministry

Beyond a new recognition of the key missional significance of school chaplaincy, a clear understanding of its present extent and the establishment of a positive policy and active strategy for the further development of school chaplaincy both within and beyond church schools, what other changes are needed?

One major and fundamental change in assumption and outlook needed is a shift from a parish-centred understanding of ministry to a more diverse and multi-contextual one. The Church of England cannot afford to keep all its eggs in the one parochial basket. Realizing this, the *Mission-Shaped Church* movement (Cray 2004) has over the past ten years encouraged the establishment of various 'fresh expressions' of church – alternative ways of 'being church' in the postmodern context – and there has been an emphasis on church planting and church growth. Though this movement has seen some success (Archbishops' Council 2014) as well as prompting a strong reassertion of the parochial model (Davison and Milbank 2010), what remains striking is the absence from the discussion of any realization of the relevance of the chaplaincy model of ministry. For all the former Archbishop of Canterbury's commendation of a 'mixed economy' of mission and ministry models, the Church appears to have concentrated on either the parochial model or what may appear to be valiant but modish and possibly short-lived 'fresh expressions'. The Church urgently needs to appreciate the vitality and utility – as well as the cost-effectiveness – of the chaplaincy mode of ministry, one that is adaptive to a whole range of contexts, of which schools is only one.

Changes in direction: reviewing clergy training and careers

This leads directly to the question of clergy training. It is a truism that clergy training is built on the assumption that becoming a vicar within the parochial system is the major – perhaps the only – serious vocation to ordination. But where a significant proportion of clergy are already employed in chaplaincy (Todd et al. 2014) it is surely time to reshape the assumptions both of clergy selection and training. Whether the tradition is evangelical or catholic, current clergy training courses appear to assume that preparation for ministry – either as grounding in the Scriptures or as priestly formation – will lead to a 'title' curacy in a parish under the direction of the incumbent, and thence to a parish incumbency. There is little recognition in the training process of the distinctive ministry of chaplaincy, although as one college principal has recently said, there is little doubt that many of his trainees will at some later point become chaplains in one context or another. That this is the case should surely prompt the Church to reshape its training of clergy on a more multi-contextual basis: clergy are not solely 'vicars' but rather people called to priestly ministry in a range of contexts – not least as self-supporting ministers in many occupational contexts and chaplains in a host of societal situations.

Needing revision also is the set of assumptions governing clergy career paths. It is now becoming accepted that transfer into the clerical profession from other professional backgrounds may bring valuable life-experience to the Church, so that the idea of practising as, for example, a lawyer and then becoming ordained and serving as a vicar is no longer that unusual. What remains less accepted, if the testimony of practising school chaplains is accurate, is the idea of moving into and out of school chaplaincy, particularly in the independent sector. There is a widespread sense among school chaplains that becoming a school chaplain may be a route of no return, although one chaplain responding to our national survey did report that his bishop wanted him to return to 'proper ministry'

in the parochial context. What would surely enrich both parochial and chaplaincy ministry is the idea that transfer from one
ministerial context to another would be positively beneficial to
the Church's mission, as ministerial perspectives and understandings were broadened by the experience of different contexts.

Changes in direction: *episcope*, support and development

Chaplaincy in schools exists in the highly professionalized context of the education system, and those serving as chaplains
deserve to receive from the institutional Church an equiva-
lent degree of professional support to that available to their
teacher colleagues. In effect, what this means is that chaplains
in schools should be subject to oversight and review – as well
as being supported by a system of pastoral supervision – and
enabled to develop professionally. The question of oversight –
episcope – is important. A chaplain employed by a school is
clearly under the direction of the school – hence the earlier-quoted
chaplain's sense of accountability to the head (see page 126) –
but is also a licensed representative of the Church. To this extent
such chaplains need to be confident that either personally or
through a senior colleague the bishop who grants the licence to
minister will at the very least be aware of what they are doing
and how they are coping with the demands of their chaplaincy
role. All this assumes that the chaplain's job description is clear
and comprehensive and that there is a fully professional grasp
of the dual accountability of the chaplain to the school and
the wider Church; and it implies that there will be a regular
system of review in place, and also that either the bishop or
a senior colleague will take active pastoral responsibility for
the chaplain, keeping in touch with the chaplain and offering
appropriate support.

The professional and personal development of chaplains
in school is a further issue. One worrying outcome of the
national survey was that responding chaplains seemed to give
little priority to higher level theological study, as if their initial

theological training had provided all the resource needed for active ministry. It is unclear whether this is a characteristic of clergy generally, but in the context of the education profession, where the assumption of masters-level qualification for all is becoming prevalent, it seems a matter of concern that chaplains are not actively seeking higher levels of theological competence and expertise. This is not to assume that theological study itself is inevitably linked to ministerial effectiveness, but in a post-Christian educational context where the young are alert to the varied intellectual challenges to belief, it seems strange that active ministers are not seeking further intellectual development through higher-level study. One of the changes needed to the culture of school chaplaincy is a greater emphasis on continuing professional development, whether that is seen primarily in intellectual/theological terms or in terms of ongoing personal/spiritual formation. The availability of suitably tailored and compelling higher-level training and development for chaplains in school needs to be a priority for those who plan the ongoing ministerial development of clergy, and this remains true also for lay chaplains: access to suitable development opportunities should be open to both clergy and laity.

Changes of culture such as these would help chaplains working in schools to feel more part of the national mission of the Church, rather than being peripheral to it. The alarming sense of detachment voiced by many chaplains responding to the national survey may at one level reflect a deliberately chosen context felt to be less mired in ecclesiastical officialdom than 'mainstream' parish ministry: some spheres of chaplaincy have been described as populated by 'refugees' from the parish system (Hancocks et al. 2008). But if the mission of the Church to the young – a spiritually under-resourced generation, remote from the culture and belief of the Church – is to be effective, then the cadre of school chaplains needs to be personally and institutionally resourced in a better way. School chaplains evince a strong and compelling sense of personal vocation to work with the young, and see their ministry as potentially transformative. What needs to change is the current shortfall in support and development for this ministry, so that those entering and working in it can be assured both that the Church is aware of their ministry and values it as a key part of the overall mission of the Church to the nation, and that they will be adequately supported and able to develop in it both professionally and personally.

Conclusion

School chaplaincy, as a 'ministry of presence', is the Church's most likely point of direct ministerial contact with the young in our post-Christian society. With pastoral care at its heart, chaplaincy in schools is a potentially transformative ministry for the post-millennium young who come within its sphere and who suffer as a generation a deficit of spiritual capital. Chaplains have the opportunity to minister to the young as representatives of Christ and his Church, and are recognized, research shows, as those who may be 'a mini-Jesus' to them. They minister according to the pattern of Christ, and in offering disinterested care and support follow his example. They also have the task of opening up the sacred sphere for the young through the ministry of word and sacrament, and of enabling the young to find their identity through becoming linked with the 'chain of memory' that is the Church. This ministry now requires better recognition, support and encouragement, and needs to be extended on a full-time basis into all church secondary schools, and then beyond. The future of this generation – not to mention that of the Church itself – is at stake.

References

Abbott, W. M. (ed.), 1966, *The Documents of Vatican II*, Piscataway, NJ: New Century.

Accord Coalition, 2014, http://accordcoalition.org.uk/.

Anderson, L., 1968, *If . . .* [Film directed by Lindsay Anderson], UK: Paramount Films.

Archbishops Council, 2014, *From Anecdote to Evidence: Findings from the Church Growth Research Programme 2011–2013*, London: Church of England.

Archdiocese of Southwark, 2007, *Guidelines for School and College Chaplaincy*, London: Archdiocese of Southwark.

Armstrong, K., 2009, *The Case for God: What Religion Really Means*, London: Bodley Head.

Atwell, R. (ed.), 2004, *Celebrating the Saints: Daily Spiritual Readings to accompany the Calendars of The Church of England, The Church of Ireland, The Scottish Episcopal Church and The Church in Wales*, Norwich: Canterbury Press.

Avis, P., 2003, *A Church Drawing Near: Spirituality and Mission in a Post-Christian Culture*, London and New York: T. & T. Clark.

Avis, P., 2005, *A Ministry Shaped by Mission*, London and New York: T. & T. Clark.

Bailey, E., 1998, *Implicit Religion: An Introduction*, London: Middlesex University Press.

Baker, C. and Skinner, H., 2006, *Faith in Action: The Dynamic Connection between Spiritual and Religious Capital*, Rugby: William Temple Foundation.

Ballard, P., 2009, 'Locating Chaplaincy: A Theological Note', *Crucible*, July–September 2009, pp. 18–24.

Bates, L., 2014, 'Everyday Sexism', http://everydaysexism.com/.

BBC News, 2014, 'David Cameron risks "alienation", public figures claim', www.bbc.co.uk/news/uk-27099700.

Beattie, T., 2007, *The New Atheists: The Twilight of Reason and the War on Religion*, London: Darton, Longman & Todd.

Benedict XVI, 2009, www.vatican.va/special/anno_sac/index_en.html.

Bhatti, D., Cameron, H., Duce, C., Sweeney, J. and Watkins, C., 2008, *Living Church in the Global City: Theology in Practice*, London: Heythrop College.

Brierley, P., 2014, www.brierleyconsultancy.com/.

British Association for Counselling and Psychotherapy, 2014, www.bacp.co.uk/.

Brown, C. G., 2001, *The Death of Christian Britain: Understanding Secularisation, 1800–2000*, Abingdon, New York: Routledge.

Bruce, S., 2002, *God is Dead: Secularisation in the West*, Maldon, MA; Oxford; Carlton, Victoria: Blackwell.

Bunting, M., 2014, 'There really is a crisis in our children's mental health', *The Guardian*, 20 May 2014.

Cameron, H., Bhatti, D., Duce, C., Sweeney, J. and Watkins, C., 2010, *Talking about God in Practice*, London: SCM Press.

Camp, M., 2014, *The Public Face of God: Chaplaincy in Anglican Secondary Schools in England and Wales*, London: Archbishops' Council Education Division.

Campbell, A. V. (ed.), 1987, *A Dictionary of Pastoral Care*, London: SPCK.

Caperon, J., 2011, *School Chaplaincy: What Does Research Tell Us?*, Cuddesdon: The Bloxham Project and OxCEPT.

Catholic Education Service, 2004, *A Guide to the Employment of Lay Chaplains in Schools and Colleges*, London: CES.

Chadwick, H., 1967, *The Early Church*, Harmondsworth: Penguin Books.

Chadwick, P., 2012, *The Church School of the Future*, London: Church of England Archbishops' Council Education Division.

The Children's Society, 2013, *The Good Childhood Report 2013 – A Summary of our Findings*, London: Children's Society.

Collins-Mayo, S. and Dandelion, P. (eds), 2010, *Religion and Youth*, Farnham, Surrey; Burlington, VT: Ashgate.

Collins-Mayo, S., Mayo, B., Nash, S. and Cocksworth, C., 2010, *The Faith of Generation Y*, London: Church House Publishing.

Crace, J., 2010, 'Humanist chaplains head to the UK', *The Guardian*, 26 January 2010.

Crawford, C. and Jin, W., 2014, 'Payback time? Student debt and loan repayments: what will the 2012 reforms mean for graduates?', London: Institute for Fiscal Studies.

Cray, G., 2004, *Mission-Shaped Church: Church Planting and Fresh Expressions of Church in a Changing Context*, London: Church House Publishing.

Davie, G., 1994, *Religion in Britain since 1945: Believing Without Belonging*, Oxford and Cambridge, MA: Blackwell.

Davison, A. and Milbank, A., 2010, *For the Parish: A Critique of Fresh Expressions*, London: SCM Press.

Dawkins, R., 2006, *The God Delusion*, London: Transworld Publishers.

Day, A., 2010, '"Believing in Belonging": An Exploration of Young People's Social Contexts and Constructions of Belief', in Collins-Mayo, S. and Dandelion, P. (eds), *Religion and Youth*, Farnham, Surrey; Burlington, VT: Ashgate.

Dearing, L., 2001, *The Way Ahead: Church of England Schools in the New Millennium*, London: Archbishop's Council.

Department for Education, 2013, 'Schools, pupils and their characteristics: January 2013', London: DFE.

Diocese of Portsmouth, 2009, 'Understanding the role of school chaplain', Portsmouth: Diocese of Portsmouth.

Donnelly, C., 2000, 'In Pursuit of School Ethos', *British Journal of Educational Studies* 48, pp. 134–54.

Dransfield, S., 2014, *A Tale of Two Britains: Inequality in the UK*, London: Oxfam GB.

Eagleton, T., 2014, *Culture and the Death of God*, New Haven, CT: Yale University Press.

Ekklesia, 2007, *United we stand? A report on current conflicts between Christian Unions and Students' Unions*, London: Ekklesia.

Eliot, T. S., 1963, *Collected Poems 1909–1962*, London: Faber & Faber.

Fowler, J. W., 1981, *Stages of Faith: The Psychology of Human Development and the Quest for Meaning*, New York: Harper & Row.

Francis, L. J. and Kay, W. K., 1995, *Teenage Religion and Values*, London: Gracewing.

Francis, L. J. and Robbins, M., 2005, *Urban Hope and Spiritual Health: The Adolescent Voice*, Peterborough: Epworth.

Fraser, G., 2014, 'Loose Canon', *The Guardian*, 31 May 2014.

Fukuyama, F., 1992, *The End of History and the Last Man*, London: Penguin Books.

Grayling, A. C., 2007, *Against All Gods: Six Polemics on Religion and an Essay on Kindness*, London: Oberon Books.

Hancocks, G., Sherborne, J. and Swift, C., 2008, '"Are They Refugees?" Why Church of England Male Clergy Enter Healthcare Chaplaincy', *Practical Theology* 1, pp. 163–79.

Hay, D., 1998, *The Spirit of the Child*, London: HarperCollins.

Hebert, G., 1961, *Liturgy and Society: The Function of the Church in the Modern World*, London: Faber & Faber.

Heelas, P. and Woodhead, L., 2005, *The Spiritual Revolution: Why Religion is Giving Way to Spirituality*, Malden, MA; Oxford; Carlton, Victoria: Blackwell.

Hervieu-Léger, D., 2000, *Religion as a Chain of Memory*, Cambridge and Maldon, MA.: Polity.

Hick, J., 1974, *Evil and the God of Love*, London: Collins.

Hitchens, C., 2007, *God is Not Great: How Religion Poisons Everything*, New York and London: Warner Books and Atlantic Books.

Holman, M., 2010, *'Put out into the deep': Address to the Association of Catholic Chaplains in Education*, London: Heythrop College.

Holness, M., 2014a, 'Challenge to daily assemblies', *Church Times*, 3 July 2014.

Holness, M., 2014b, 'Rethink collective worship', *Church Times*, 10 July 2014.

Holness, M., 2014c, 'Review signals drive to improve standard of RE', *Church Times*, 19 September 2014.

Hopkins, G. M., 1947, *Poems of Gerard Manley Hopkins*, Oxford: Oxford University Press.

Hughes, T., 2008, *Tom Brown's Schooldays*, London: Oxford University Press.

Hume, B., 1997, 'The Church's Mission in Education', *Partners in Mission*, London: Catholic Education Service.

Hunter, R. J. (ed.), 1990, 2005, *Dictionary of Pastoral Care and Counselling*, Nashville: Abingdon Press.

James, O., 2007, *Affluenza: How to be Successful and Stay Sane*, London: Random House.

Jones, C., Wainwright, G. and Yarnold, E. (eds), 1980, *The Study of Liturgy*, London: SPCK.

Leach, J. and Paterson, M., 2010, *Pastoral Supervision: A Handbook*. London: SCM Press.

Loades, A. and MacSwain, R. (eds), 2006, *The Truth-Seeking Heart: Austin Farrer and His Writings*, Norwich: Canterbury Press.

Lyall, D., 2001, *The Integrity of Pastoral Care*, London: SPCK.

MacCulloch, D., 2009, *A History of Christianity: The First Three Thousand Years*, London: Allen Lane.

Maclure, J. S., 1965, *Educational Documents: England and Wales 1816 to the Present Day*, London: Methuen.

Malik, S., 2014, 'The dependent generation: Half young European adults live with their parents', *The Guardian*, 24 March 2014.

Marsh, R., 1987, 'School Chaplaincy', in A. V. Campbell (ed.), *A Dictionary of Pastoral Care*, London: SPCK.

McGrath, A. and Collicutt, J., 2007, *The Dawkins Delusion? Atheist Fundamentalism and the Denial of the Divine*, London: SPCK.

McKeone, M., 1993, *Wasting Time in School: Secondary School Chaplaincy – A Story and a Handbook*, Slough and Maynooth: St Paul's Press.

REFERENCES

McLaughlin, T., 2005, 'The Educative Importance of Ethos', *British Journal of Educational Studies* 53, pp. 306–25.

Moreton, C., 2014, 'Rowan Williams: I didn't really want to be Archbishop', www.telegraph.co.uk/news/features/10789740/Rowan-Williams-I-didnt-really-want-to-be-Archbishop.html.

Morisy, A., 2004, *Journeying Out: A New Approach to Christian Mission*, London and New York: Continuum.

Morisy, A., 2006, 'Mapping the Mixed Economy', in S. Croft (ed.), *The Future of the Parish System*, London: Church House Publishing.

Murphy, S., 2004, 'A Study of Pupils' Perceptions and Experiences of School Chaplaincy', in J. E. Norman (ed.), *At the Heart of Education: School Chaplaincy and Pastoral Care*, Dublin: Veritas.

Newsome, D., 1961, *Godliness and Good Learning: Four Studies on a Victorian Ideal*, London: Cassell.

Niebuhr, H. R., 1951, *Christ and Culture*, New York: Harper & Row.

Ofsted, 2004, *Promoting and Evaluating Pupils' Spiritual, Moral, Social and Cultural Development*, London: Ofsted.

Ofsted, 2013, *Religious Education: Realising the Potential*, London: Ofsted.

Pattison, S., 1997, *Pastoral Care and Liberation Theology*, London: SPCK.

Pattison, S., 2008, 'Is Pastoral Care Dead in a Mission-led Church?', *Practical Theology* 1, pp. 7–10.

Percy, M., 2005, *Engaging with Contemporary Culture: Christianity, Theology and the Concrete Church*, Aldershot and Burlington, VT: Ashgate.

Percy, M., 2006, *Clergy: The Origin of Species*, London and New York: Continuum.

Percy, M., 2013, *Anglicanism: Confidence, Commitment and Communion*, Farnham and Burlington, VT: Ashgate.

The Prince's Trust, 2011, *Broke, not Broken: Tackling Youth Poverty and the Aspiration Gap*, London: The Prince's Trust.

Purves, A., 2001, *Pastoral Theology in the Classical Tradition*, Louisville, KY and London: Westminster John Knox Press.

Rahner, K., 1963, *Mission and Grace*, London and New York: Sheed & Ward.

Ramsey, I., 1970, *The Fourth R: the Durham Report on Religious Education*, London: The National Society.

Rees, G., Francis, L. J. and Robbins, M., 2005, *Spiritual Health and the Well-Being of Urban Young People*, London: The Commission on Urban Life and Faith and University of Wales, Bangor; The Children's Society.

Richardson, R. and Chapman, J., 1973, *Images of Life: Problems of Religious Belief and Human Relations in Schools*, London: SCM Press.

Rowson, J., 2014, *Spiritualise: Revitalising Spirituality to Address 21st Century Challenges*, London: Royal Society of Arts.

Ryan, B., 2015, *A Very Modern Ministry: Chaplaincy in the UK*, London: Theos.

Sabina, C., Wolak, J. and Finkelhor, D., 2008, 'The Nature and Dynamics of Internet Pornography Exposure for Youth', *Cyberpsychology and Behaviour* 11.6.

Savage, S., Collins-Mayo, S., Mayo, B. and Cray, G., 2006, *Making Sense of Generation Y: The World View of 15–25-year olds*, London: Church House Publishing.

Schoolswork, 2014, http://schoolswork.co.uk.

Scripture Union, 2014, www.scriptureunion.org.uk/8.id.

Sharma, S. and Hopkins, P., 2013, https://research.ncl.ac.uk/youngpeo ple/workingpapersseries/racereligionandmigration/Paper%202%20 -%20Spiritual%20well-being%20and%20young%20people's%20 resilience%20in%20times%20of%20austerity.pdf.

Slater, V., 2013, 'The Fresh Significance of Chaplaincy for the Mission and Ministry of the Church in England: Three Case Studies in Community Contexts', DProf. thesis, Cambridge: Anglia Ruskin University.

Spencer, N., 2002, *A Christian Perspective on Human Flourishing*, London: Theos.

Taylor, C., 1991, *The Ethics of Authenticity*, Cambridge, MA: Harvard University Press.

Taylor, C., 2007, *A Secular Age*, Cambridge, MA: Harvard University Press.

Thompson, Clive, 2013, 'My 250 texts a day', *The Guardian* 5 October 2013.

Threlfall-Holmes, M. and Newitt, M., 2011, *Being a Chaplain*, London: SPCK.

Todd, A., Slater, V. and Dunlop, S., 2014, *The Church of England's Involvement in Chaplaincy*, Cardiff and Cuddesdon: Cardiff Centre for Chaplaincy Studies and Oxford Centre for Ecclesiology and Practical Theology.

Topping, A., 2013, 'Self-harm sites and cyberbullying: the threat to children from web's dark side', *The Guardian*, 11 March 2014.

UCCF, 2014, www.uccf.org.uk/.

UNICEF, 2013, *Report Card 11: Child Well-being in Rich Countries*, London: UNICEF UK.

Watts, F., Nye, R. and Savage, S., 2002, *Psychology for Christian Ministry*, Abingdon and New York: Routledge.

Weardon, G., 2014, 'Oxfam: 85 richest people as wealthy as poorest half of the world', *The Guardian*, 20 January 2014.

Westminster Faith Debates, 2014, http://faithdebates.org.uk/.

Williams, R., 2004, 'A Culture of Hope? Priorities and Vision in Church Schools', *Journal of the Association of Anglican Secondary School Heads*, February 2004.

Williams, R., 2014, 'T. S. Eliot's Christian Society and the current political crisis', *The Journal of the T. S. Eliot Society* 2014, pp. 1–12.

Woodhead, L., 2010, 'Epilogue', in Collins-Mayo, S. and Dandelion, P. (eds), *Religion and Youth*, Farnham, Surrey; Burlington, VT: Ashgate.

Index

Augustine, St 8, 95
Avis, Paul 11–12, 78, 85, 86, 95

Ballard, Paul 50, 70
Bloxham Project ix, x, xii, 14, 51–2, 53, 60, 67, 82, 83, 99, 109, 115, 132, 133
Bourdieu, Pierre 47, 112

chaplain(cy) vii, ix, xii, 1–16, 34, 50, 51, 52, 53, 54–8, 61, 63–4, 65, 66, 68–70, 73–9, 82, 87, 94–8, 99, 100, 110, 115, 121, 123, 130, 131, 135, 138, 140
and Church *see* Church on chaplaincy
development of chaplaincy 4, 13–16
embedded 59–60, 62, 65
humanist 1, 5, 6, 8
interfaith 1
job description 72, 73, 124–5, 129, 138
as intermediary and mediator 63, 71, 72, 120
lay 14, 89, 102, 119, 139
multi-faith xiii, 3, 14, 20, 21
non-faith 1, 5–6, 15–16, 21, 78
other faith 5–6, 10, 15–16, 21, 32, 41, 77, 78, 118
'para' viii, 60, 65, 122, 127–8, 134

priest 55, 56, 59, 71
as representative of Christ 60–2, 65–6, 67–9, 115
as role model 63, 69
school viii, ix–xii, 14–15, 17, 20, 41, 43–9, 50–66, 67–8, 69–72, 73–4, 75–81, 83–5, 86, 88–9, 90–5, 96, 99, 100–1, 103–5, 108–11, 113, 114, 115–20, 124, 125–30, 131–9
teacher x, 13, 15, 54, 58–9, 65, 69, 122–4
tradition 5, 14, 15, 123, 127
training and development xii, 2, 5, 13–16, 88–9, 90, 132, 134–40
volunteering 5, 15, 59–60
Chaucer, Geoffrey viii, 2–3, 10
Christ xi, 3, 9, 10, 11–12, 16, 43, 45, 46–7, 50, 53, 54, 55, 56, 62, 63, 65–7, 68–9, 70, 81, 97, 98, 103, 105, 107, 113, 114, 115, 128, 129, 133, 135, 140
see also Jesus
Christian(ity)
medieval 3
tradition viii, xii, 10, 31, 32, 33, 34, 36, 43–4, 47, 70, 84, 91, 93, 96
see also community, Christian; community, post-Christian; faith, Christian; identity, Christian; mission, Christian

148

INDEX

Pattison, Stephen 7–8, 16, 53, 75, 84, 86
Percy, Martyn 9–10, 55, 63
pornography 26
post-Christian *see* community, post-Christian
post-millennium *see* society, post-millennium generation

Rahner, Karl 3
religious literacy 34, 39, 64, 108–10, 112, 123, 135
religious socialization 48, 49, 78, 110
Roman Catholic Church 3, 14, 41, 45–50, 53, 104, 134
 schools 14, 41–2 45–7, 49, 50, 53, 104, 134
Runcie, Archbishop Robert 109, 119

Sacrament(al) 12, 16, 53, 65, 98, 103, 129, 131, 140
 school(s) 41, 43, 45, 46–9, 50–66, 69–71, 77–80, 88–9, 91, 93–5, 100–1, 103–5, 108, 109, 110, 112, 113, 114, 115–30
 faith 42, 43
 identity 42, 44, 45, 73, 74, 77, 78
 Sunday 30, 133
 worship 100, 103, 106–8, 110, 111, 112–13, 114
 see also chaplaincy, school; Church schools
Scripture(s) 97–8, 111, 118, 137
society
 international 22–2
 post-millennium generation 8–9, 16, 17, 23, 24–6, 27–9, 30–1, 32–3, 34, 48–9, 140
 post-modern 136
 post-war 36, 134
 see also community; culture

spiritual
 capital 32–3, 34–5, 36, 43, 49, 112–13, 140
 development xii, 34–5, 40, 48, 49, 50, 70, 107, 113, 115
spirituality xii, 10, 20, 29, 31, 40, 46–8, 57, 78–9, 93, 96, 104, 106, 111, 114, 119
 personal 100, 110, 116
state, the xii, 33, 34–9, 49, 79, 87

Taylor, Charles 19, 37, 92
theology ix, xi, 11, 47, 60, 63, 66, 67, 80, 104, 119, 132
 chaplaincy 46, 53, 62, 85, 134
 Imago Dei (image of God) 12, 61
 liberation 7, 8–9, 16
 worship 102–3

Vatican Council, Second 11

well-being 7–9, 28–9, 86–7, 90, 93, 112, 115
 see also young people, well-being
Westminster Faith Debates 21–2
William Temple Foundation 112
Williams, Archbishop Rowan 20, 114, 135
worship x, 2, 3–4, 12, 13, 14, 30, 33, 35–40, 43, 49, 50, 52, 72, 74, 77, 78, 79, 80, 86, 99, 101–2, 104–5, 109, 114, 115–16, 122, 123, 128, 132, 133, 135
 school 100, 103, 106–8, 110, 111, 112–13, 114

young people vi, vii–viii, ix–xii, 8–9, 10, 25–6, 28, 29, 30–1, 32, 43, 48, 91, 92, 95, 104
 anxiety and depression 28, 33, 34, 46, 48, 49, 92